Taylor malone

MW01042770

PROFESSIONALLY *polished*

Business Etiquette Savvy for Today's Competitive Market

Dallas Teague-Snider

Tendril Press

Aurora, CO

Professionally Polished:
Business Etiquette Savvy for Today's Competitive Market
Copyright © 2009 by Dallas Teague-Snider. All Rights Reserved.
www.ProfessionallyPolished.com

Published by Tendril Press™
www.TendrilPress.com
PO 441110
Aurora, CO 80044
303.696.9227
Educational & Corporate Quantity Discounts available

ISBN 978-0-9822394-1-4

10 9 8 7 6 5 4 3 2 First Publishing: 2009

Author Photo by:
Omni Studios, Liesa Cole

Art Direction, Book Design and Cover Design © 2009. All Rights Reserved by
A. J. Images Inc. Business Design & Publishing Center
www.AJImagesinc.com — 303•696•9227
Info@AJImagesInc.com

Contents

Foreword

Dallas Teague-Snider says that in the corporate jungle, it's not the lions and tigers that get you, it's the mosquitoes. For her, the mosquitoes are the details, or more to the point, manners, and finally here's a book that enumerates them, teaches them, and elevates them to their proper level.

Professionally Polished is a book you should read and then re-read again and again. It's chock full of advice on making a great and lasting impression—everything from how to greet someone in a foreign country and cell phone etiquette to which way to pass a dinner dish and where to stow your purse during an interview.

Thank you, Dallas. If only a handful of people take this book to heart (and no doubt, there will be many, many more), you will have made the world a better, and much more brilliant place.

— Simon T. Bailey, author of
Release Your Brilliance

Introduction

I stood steadfast at the hotel's front desk, firmly denying a client's unreasonable demand. His robust stature towered over me, and he glared down at me as if I were an ant that needed to be stomped. His body language indicated he believed he would eventually get his way.

Having carefully reviewed the contract, it was clear I could not honor his request. I did, however, suggest a reasonable alternative and even offered to make a call to his company to clear up any possible miscommunication. The guest suddenly decided he could live with the situation as is, yet he was obviously displeased.

Feeling quite proud, I secretly congratulated myself for handling the situation perfectly and not allowing another's behavior dictate how I would react. I was a rock.

I rounded the corner from behind the front desk and strutted through the lobby to the ladies' room. After a quick check in the mirror, I smoothed the front of my soft, flowing skirt and reentered the lobby. I chassed right past the client on my way back to the front desk.

I looked ahead to see my co-workers' eyes as wide as saucers. They motioned quickly for me to get behind the front desk and immediately led me to the office area, out of view of the lobby. Suddenly, my self-satisfied feeling sank to embarrassment when I realized that I had inadvertently trapped the back of my skirt inside my panty hose.

I was mortified and lingered behind the front desk until the client left the lobby. I imagine he was thinking, *Who got the last laugh now? Forget the free room, I got a free show!* As troublesome as that client had been, he did teach me a valuable lesson—never leave the restroom without making sure everything is as you intend it to be.

Have you ever had an embarrassing moment on the job? If so, I bet you will never let it happen again. I like to call these dubious gifts *life lessons.* This book is loaded with real-life stories of etiquette gaffes and snafus from business professionals in various fields—life lessons from myself and others who have generously shared their faux pas and fumbles. Some of these stories will make you laugh, others may make you cringe.

If you can learn your own lessons with an attitude of lightness and self-forgiveness, it will be an easy road. I encourage you to be gentle with yourself as you learn business etiquette mastery and remember we all make mistakes; the key is to learn from them and move on.

You will learn the tools necessary to help you avoid these costly mistakes and make your best impression. One way or another, you will learn. It is my hope that *Professionally Polished* will help you avoid most of the etiquette pitfalls that await the unarmed and uninformed.

In business today, it is crucial to a person's overall success to understand proper business etiquette and protocol guidelines. With an understanding of appropriate behavior and manners in the workplace, you will have the knowledge that will set you apart from your competition.

Business etiquette savvy guides us in communication and establishes effective interactions that are the building blocks of successful relationships. Regardless of age, gender, income, educational level or marital status, each of us will be judged based on our social skills and how we handle tricky situations. The perception camera is always rolling. Wherever you go, you're on!

When you least expect it, your behavior can positively or negatively affect your future. During the mid-90's, I was in transition and had taken a temporary position at a resort. My role was to market and increase the membership of an upscale, invitation-only golf course. As part of our marketing efforts, my colleague and I attended a PGA Golf event to represent the resort. Much to my surprise, someone sent a letter to the general manager that led the resort to create a "permanent" job for me in the sales department. The letter is provided at the end of this introduction.

In today's competitive environment, companies that fail to emphasize and nurture business etiquette intelligence often pay for it with lost revenue. There is a saying that where people lack vision, they will perish. This is true for companies as well. Customer service is not optional; it's a tool for survival.

A recent survey found that employees are behaving more rudely to their co-workers and colleagues. Managers know, cutbacks in common courtesy and kindness result in greater employee turnover, which hurts the bottom line. As this is a growing concern, individuals who master business etiquette skills will increasingly be recognized as a valued company asset with an edge over their co-workers.

This book reveals the critical areas of business etiquette that, once mastered, will facilitate success in your career. As a practical guide, it will help you interact effectively with your colleagues, customers and supervisors. From body language and non-verbal cues to electronic communication, you will find the basic principles that will put your career on a vertical track.

Whether you are seated in the boardroom or applying for your first job after college, these skills will give you the confidence you need to be your best self. After reading this book, you will be armed with the business etiquette principles that will aid you in gaining trust and earning new business, and your co-workers and superiors will respect you. Every minute you don't have the information is costing your future success, so let's get started. Your best self begins today.

Warm regards,
Dallas Teague-Snider, CMP
Founder and President
Make Your Best Impression
www.makeyourbestimpression.com

MICHAEL C. TRUFANT
GENERAL MANAGER, CELLULAR ONE
P.O. BOX 40565
BATON ROUGE, LOUISIANA 70835
_____
(504) 291-5990

04/27/97

Mr. Reed Pulan
The Marriot Grand Hotel
One Grand Boulevard
Point Clear, AL 36564-0639

Dear Mr. Pulan:

I had the pleasure of attending the Freeport-McDermott Golf Classic April 4th in New Orleans.

While attending the tournament I had the pleasure meeting one of your associates, Dallas Teague. I came to find out the she was there representing memberships in your Lakewood Golf Club.

I just wanted to drop you a note and tell you it was a pleasure to meet her and her associate. They were excellent representatives of Lakewood(of which I have played). They were polite, cordial, and represented The Grand very well. While they were selling, they acted in a most professional manner. That takes skill. I thought I'd pass along the positive feedback. *Please pass it on to them.*

See you at The Grand! With best wishes,

DALLAS —
GREAT JOB!
KEEP

e-mail: mctrufant@cellonebr.com   fax: 504-291-9801

Dallas,
Thanks!
David Clark

CC: DAVID MONROE

Professionally Polished
Dallas Teague-Snider

Chapter 1

Keep It Simply Savvy

It doesn't take money to have class.

— Louise De Angelo Betancourt
My Beloved Grandmother

Why Should You Care About Etiquette?

What is the difference between two individuals competing for the same job, client, or business deal when they have the same background, education, technical skills, and a similar product or service?

In business, the worst advice anyone can offer is "Don't sweat the small stuff." The difference between business success and failure is in the details. Attention to the small stuff equals big business opportunities.

It takes three to five seconds to make a first impression; therefore, as potential business relationships are considered, a candidate's appearance and demonstrated verbal communication skills create an instant and lasting impression. By presenting a *Professionally Polished* image, you will evoke a favorable reaction from clients and potential employers and also build self-esteem and confidence.

You've heard the term, "You never get a second chance to make a first impression." Well, it is often true, and a negative image can block you from your true potential. Long uncombed hair, casual attire, visible tattoos and body piercing is an appropriate look for a rock concert, but not in business. You have a choice: you can adjust your professional style or consider changing your career. As a professional, you want your image to convey a feeling of comfort and confidence about your skills and knowledge.

Often the term etiquette brings to mind something that is stuffy or arrogant. Actually, etiquette in its truest form is the way you make others feel. Think for a moment about someone you consider successful. What characteristics or traits does this person possess? Do they make you feel like you are the most important person in the room? Do they seem to have an uncanny ability to connect with people? The truth is that 85% of our success is based on our social skills. The great news is that these skills can be learned.

In the business and professional world, it is crucial to a person's success to practice proper business etiquette and protocol. Using appropriate behavior and manners in the workplace will set you apart from your competition. Business etiquette intelligence guides us in communication and establishes effective interactions that are the building blocks of relationships. Regardless of age, gender, income, educational levels or marital status, each of us will be judged based on our social skills and how we react in any given situation.

When a company neglects these skills as an important part of the culture, the cost is lost customers and revenue. Companies are beginning to take note that a lack of business etiquette, common courtesy and kindness is also a factor in employee turnover, which affects their bottom-line as well. Business etiquette savvy will help you be recognized as someone who has both the technical ability to perform a job and the social skills to ensure the job gets done smoothly—a valuable asset for any company.

"What is Etiquette?"

Most of us hear the terms *etiquette* and *protocol* now and then; however, like many words, we rarely think about the origin or how the meaning has evolved over time. In the days of Louis XIV, aristocrats had a bad habit of trampling through the gardens. At the behest of the King, the gardener put up signs or *etiquets* to ward them off. Common sense to one is not common sense to another, and many aristocrats were ignoring the signs. The King finally had to issue a declaration that no one could go beyond the bounds of *etiquets*. The meaning later expanded to include all rules regarding what to do and where to stand at court functions.

Etiquette continues to evolve, but at its essence, it still means "keep off the grass." By practicing the rules and guidelines of etiquette, we open up the opportunity to acquire authentic self-confidence and develop happy relationships.

If you grew up before the 1960s, chances are you had etiquette training, either in public or private school, or in one of the popular charm schools. The cultural revolution of the 60's and 70's marked a decline in the popularity of etiquette education, and although it is once again on the rise, most adults today have had no formal etiquette training, as evidenced by the increase in rude behavior. While widespread rudeness makes day-to-day life more challenging, those who bother to develop even basic etiquette skills will distinguish themselves as extraordinary people and coveted workers.

"What is Protocol?"

The term "protocol" is derived from two Greek words, *Pr'otos* meaning "the first" and *kola* meaning "glue". By the 19th century, the French term *Protocole diplomatique* or *protcole de la chancellerie* referred to a body of rules to be observed in all ceremonies and official interaction in the field of diplomacy among nations. Today, the term protocol maintains its standing as an international code of diplomatic civility, and it has made its way into the business world.

In the computer industry, technical standards and codes that enable communication, connection and data transfer are named "protocols." Perhaps as a result, many companies have adopted the term to describe their own codes for human behavior. Which protocols does your organization have in place to ensure smooth daily operations? What code of ethics, standard of conduct or standard operating procedures does your company embrace? A company handbook is a form of corporate protocol which delineates the rules to be followed—not to be interpreted as mere suggestions.

According to John Malloy's *Live for Success*, (William Morrow & Co, 1981), 99 out of 100 executives surveyed agree that etiquette skills are prerequisites for success in any endeavor and that the ability to demonstrate poise and social grace at a cocktail party or dinner table is at least as important as one's skill in a boardroom.

The K.I.S.S. Method: Keep it Simply Savvy!

So, how does this affect today's business professional? Now that you have a general understanding of etiquette and protocol, you can learn some dos and don'ts to help you make your best impression. It is crucial to have self-confidence and trust in your own business practices. By projecting a confident image right from the start, you can establish the groundwork for a mutually beneficial relationship.

The K.I.S.S. method is a simple three question checklist you can use for self-evaluation in any situation. Ask yourself the following questions to determine if your behavior is having a positive or negative impact on your personal brand.

- Does my behavior offend, insult, ignore or interrupt another person?
- Would I consider this behavior rude, awkward, unprofessional or tacky if I witnessed someone else doing it?
- Have I assessed the situation accurately to grasp the full implications of my actions?

Chapter 2

The First Impression

First impressions are the most lasting.

— William Congreve
English Playwright and Poet

Sixteen years ago, I was young and new on the job, slowly meeting the regional staff as travel opportunities or training events allowed. I knew, because someone had mentioned it, that two of the regional directors were African-American, and when I saw a black man at a post-training reception, I marched right up to him and extended my hand, saying "You must be Stan Boyer [name changed]!" He was gracious, but said no, he was not Stan. He was the **other** black regional director. I was mortified.

— Anonymous

What can you do in three to five seconds? One Mississippi, two Mississippi...that is not much time is it? Well, it only takes three to five seconds to make a first impression. The great news is that when you learn the nuances of business etiquette you will find that making a good first impression will become second nature, like riding a bicycle.

When an employer evaluates job applications, the candidate's appearance and demonstrated communication skills create an instant and lasting impression. Once you land a job, maintaining a positive impression evokes a favorable reaction from clients and also builds your self-esteem and confidence.

In contrast, a negative image can block your true potential. Often you do not get a second chance. As a professional, your image should convey a feeling of ease and confidence to your customers and co-workers.

First and foremost, to present yourself in the best light, keep your attitude positive. Happy, pleasant, polite people are nice to be around, and make engaging work partners. Have you ever heard the saying, "People do business with people they like."? We don't always know *why* we like someone, we just know we do. On the flip side, sometimes we get the sense that someone is difficult or untrustworthy. This is often based on a feeling that begins with a first impression.

Communication Secrets

There are three elements of communication that contribute to making your first impression your best impression. They are:

- Non-verbal communication
- Verbal communication
- Physical appearance

Non-verbal Communication

The power of non-verbal communication can be summed up in one word: charisma. Do you have it? Do you know some who has it? What is it? *Dictionary.com* defines *charisma* as "a personal attractiveness or interestingness that enables you to influence others." Think of a person you know who seems to have a way of lighting up a room, or someone whom you hold with high regard but can't quite pinpoint what makes him unique. It's charisma!

The exciting news is that you can learn some basic social skills that will help you enhance your own personal attractiveness—your personal flair, what makes you uniquely you. Just think, if your name is Steve and you make the effort to become an expert at being your best, likable, fun self. You would be operating in your personal *Steve-ness*. Here we go...

Body Language

Body language can be a powerful tool to make others predisposed to like you, or unwittingly turn them off. Subtle gestures, such as the way you stand or how you carry yourself when you enter a room, convey a lot about your confidence, credibility and self-respect.

To communicate a *Yes Attitude*, smile, widen your eyes, and show interest with a nod or a slight opening of the mouth. Arms relaxed at the sides and legs shoulder width apart also indicate that you are positively responding to the connection.

Convey confidence by steeping your fingers (fingers touching like a church steeple), keeping your hands in your coat pockets with thumbs out, or standing in proper posture with hands behind your back.

Negative signals include rolling your eyes, frowning, glaring, smirking, looking tense and sitting with your arms crossed. If you tend to cross your arms when you are cold, be conscious that your facial expressions still communicate openness and a positive attitude.

Mirroring is another great connection strategy. We naturally tend to like people who are like us. Often, we find that we choose friends with similar behaviors and interests. Mirror gestures, facial expressions, speech styles, posture, actions, beliefs and values, but be courteously subtle, lest your efforts be confused with mimicry. A person will feel comfortable when you copy his or her mannerisms indirectly, and a mutual connection will occur on a deeper level. Your main goal while mirroring is to find an authentic shared interest and build a rapport. We can find common ground with anyone if we ask the right questions.

Empathy

Your communication will prove effective when you recognize subtle signals from others. Being empathetic will help your companion feel comfortable. The secret lies in your ability to see things from the other person's point of view. People don't care how much you know until they know how much you care. During a new introduction, most people are thinking, *What do they want?* or *What's in it for me?* When you empathize with someone it allows them to retract their defense mechanisms.

To really hone this skill, practice observation and awareness to discern the best way to steer the conversation. Imagine yourself in the other person's position. Step inside their world, and your understanding will be enhanced. By giving sincere attention to others you meet, you too will benefit. Expect to meet fascinating and wonderful people. You increase your likelihood of finding great opportunities when you make a conscious choice to expect them. What you focus on will manifest and become your reality. Soon you will glean positive reactions and attitudes in your favor.

Eye Contact

Eye contact is a very important aspect of communication. Use direct eye contact between 40 to 60 percent of the time when talking with someone. More than 60 percent eye contact will make you seem aggressive and overbearing, and make others uncomfortable. Too little eye contact will make you seem insecure or shifty. Proper eye contact will establish respect and reveal your genuine interest in the other person. Below are the target areas for eye contact based on level of a relationship.

- For business- focus your gaze between the eyes and the center of the forehead.
- For social- focus your gaze between the eyes and upper mouth area.
- For intimate- you may focus your gaze between mid-face and upper chest. Never focus below the chin in business or social settings, as this is considered offensive.

Handshake

The handshake is known as the universal business greeting. Many cultures study and use the Western handshake. Used properly, it is an effective initial step to building rapport. However, it can just as easily create awkwardness if done clumsily.

Five Keys to a Stellar Business Handshake:

- Maintain a proper distance—one arm's length in the U.S.
- Stand shoulder to shoulder.
- Shake from the elbow.
- Shake firmly with a web-to-web grip, two to three smooth pumps. No dainty hands or limp wrists.
- Shake to connect, not to overpower. Firm does not mean crushing. Avoid a bone crushing grip. Our goal is connect with a person, not to hurt.

If you are working with clients from other countries, research the proper greeting for that culture. Honor foreign clients by learning their proper greeting, and this will speak volumes about your professionalism and respect for their customs.

Verbal Communication

You Know What They Say About Assumptions...

Rule #1 of verbal communication: never make assumptions.

At the ripe old age of 19, I was working as a bank teller and putting myself through college. One afternoon, a nicely appointed lady pulled her gold Mercedes up to the drive-through. As I greeted her and sent out the teller drawer, I noticed that she did not include a driver's license. I reviewed the information and kindly told Ms. Smith if she would please sign the back of her husband, Michael Smith's check, I would be happy to cash it.

She looked at me astonished and said with a stern voice "I am Michael Smith!"

I quickly replied with a smile, "Oh, I have a bisexual name too!"

At this point, my co-worker was rolling on the floor laughing. I noticed that Ms. Smith was looking at me strangely, but I didn't know why. I completed the transaction and she was on her way.

After Ms. Smith was out of view, I looked at my friend and said, "What is so funny?"

"You said you have a bisexual name!" she snorted.

"No I didn't!" I replied aghast, "I said I have a *unisex* name."

"No," she said. "That's why that customer was looking at you so surprised."

I tried to retrace how I did that, and I could only figure my brain was thinking "two", like bi-annual. That is a slip up I will never forget!

Names like Dallas, Leslie, Francis, Gene, and many others may be given to a child of either gender. When writing an email or letter, try to find out the recipient's gender before sending it. If you are still unclear, address the correspondence with their full name. For example: "Dear Leslie Brown," instead of "Dear Leslie," (which is too informal if you have never met) or "Dear Ms. Brown," (which could be the wrong gender).

Every assumption you make affords another opportunity to "open mouth, insert foot."

I was walking through the park, taking in the ambience of my 10-year high school reunion, and I came across a high school friend that I had not seen since graduation. Bright eyed and smiling, she was pushing a baby stroller. We greeted each other with a hug.

"Wow, it is so great to see you! When are you due?" The words flew out of my mouth like a bat out of a dark cave.

Her eyes darkened and her smile sank as she said, "Dee, I am not pregnant."

I vowed never to make that same mistake again, but, alas, my lesson had yet to be learned.

While attending an industry golfing event, I was hitting balls at the driving range next to a lady (a potential client) who appeared without a doubt to be "expecting." After giving this careful thought and assessing (*assuming*) she must be an older parent, I determined I should definitely acknowledge her great blessing. I was once again incorrect. I later mused: After that exchange, she probably wanted to be my client about as much as she enjoyed being mistaken for pregnant!

And then…about five years after college, I ran into one of my old college friends at a local department store. The cutest little boy sat good-humoredly in her shopping cart. I knew she had a son about my age, so of course I **assumed** and said, "Oh, is this your grandson?"

Imagine my surprise when she replied, "No, this is my son."

By now, you know the moral of these stories. Never ever assume anything! What is intended as a gesture of kindness can lead to unintentional hurt, and, even worse, can cost you a job or a relationship.

It is always best to just offer a greeting and follow the introduction guidelines covered later in this chapter and in Chapter 7. Let the other person offer the insight you need to move the conversation forward. For example: I could have said to my college friend, "Oh, what a nice surprise! Who is this little guy?"

She would then reply, "This is my son, Daniel."

Mystery solved—and no hurt feelings.

Misunderstandings happen from time to time; however, do your best to avoid making assumptions. With a little thought and skillful questioning, you can save yourself and others a lot of awkwardness and heartache. Situations rife with opportunities to make the wrong assumption include:

- An older parent with younger children
- An older women with a younger man
- A older man with a younger woman
- Adopted children with parents of a different ethnic background
- And, of course, when the other party has a *unisex* name.

Be extra mindful when approaching these situations.

Other strategies to making a *Professionally Polished* first impression: use a memorable introduction, learn the art of small talk, use proper grammar, speak clearly, and get good at the name game.

Personal Sound Bite

Prepare a brief introduction about yourself including your name, your company, products and services offered, and what role you have within the company. Think of these as your 30-, 60- and 90-second elevator speeches or commercials. Be sure your message is clear and concise.

For example: "Hello, my name is Dallas Teague-Snider, Founder of Make Your Best Impression. Our goal is to help individuals, companies and organizations make their first impression their best impression."

A natural follow up to this would be, "How does your company do that?"

"We offer seminars and personal coaching for clients looking to improve their professional skills."

These "sound bites" will either provoke more discussion or give you a solid foundation to follow up with your new contact at a later date.

Small Talk

Initiate small talk in a relaxed manner. This can be as easy as, "Isn't it a beautiful day?" or "Did you see the game last weekend?" You can approach any topic that is neutral and inoffensive. Remember, your goal is to connect and build relationships. Avoid topics such as religion, politics, diet or any other matter that seems too personal. Of course, it depends on the client and your relationship. Bottom line—use common sense.

USA Today is a great resource for breaking news and interesting topics for small talk. There is a section that covers happenings in each state. Use it as a reference when you communicate with people in locations scattered throughout the U.S.

Be careful when getting your information from the Internet. While there are many reputable sites, the emergence of social media and blogging has led to a lot of reporting without necessarily checking the facts. Be sure to get your facts straight before taking a stand on any topic that could be divisive.

Keys to small talk:

- Initiate the conversation. Consider this your responsibility.
- Ask opened-ended questions—questions that require more than a yes or no answer.
- Show interest and be interesting. Be aware of current events.
- Pause. Don't be afraid of the silence.
- Don't interrupt. Avoid the temptation to respond before the other party has finished.

Proper Grammar and Speech

Well-spoken individuals project a polished, competent image and gain a professional edge. The ability to offer your thoughts in a clear, concise manner with proper grammar and sentence structure is paramount to your success. Extremely heavy accents or overuse of regional jargon can have a negative impact on your professional image. Be wary of using acronyms or industry jargon. Ask someone you trust if it would be a wise investment for you to seek a professional who can assist you with these and other speech challenges.

Keys to improving your verbal skills:

- Mirror someone who speaks well.
- Ask for honest feedback on your speech. Do you mumble or speak too loudly?
- Invest in a professional development class.
- Never use profanity or off-color jokes in professional settings.

The Name Game

Remembering names and ensuring your name is remembered are two separate skills. You can increase your business savvy by subtly training others to remember your name, and employing strategies to deposit new names into your memory banks.

If you have a unique name, you will feel my pain. Yes, I love it now, but please. When I was growing up, JR was shot on the popular television show, *Dallas*—a 1980's night-time soap opera that revolved around a family of wealthy Texas oilmen. I wanted a name like Valerie or Lori, but no, I was Dallas, named after my grandfather. Of course, I got my share of teasing and still do from time to time. I eventually grew to appreciate my name, and, in business, it has proven to be a wonderful asset. Why? Because, people can easily relate something to my name that helps them remember it. When meeting new people, I often say, "Hi, my name is Dallas Teague-Snider. Dallas, like Texas."

I do this for two reasons: one, if I don't, they always think they have misheard my name and call me *Alice* and two; I am immediately giving them a means to remember me with a mental association.

I met a unique musician named Trena at an acting workshop. The second week of class, I referred to her as (Tree-na).

Fortunately, she replied, "It's Trena, like *Trinidad*."

I also have the opposite challenge. A person I met years ago will remember my name, and I will recognize the face, but the name escapes me.

Here are a few tips to help you remember names, or gracefully get a name you forgot:

- **Enlist a partner** – Now that I am married, my husband often attends events as my guest. I have made a deal with him that if I do not introduce him within two or three minutes, he will extend his hand and introduce himself. People will usually offer their name in response.

- **Thrice is nice** – When you are introduced to someone, try to use their name three times during your initial exchange. For example: "Hi, John. So, John, which division do you work for at Biotech? How long have you been with the company? Well, John, it was a pleasure to meet you. I hope to see you again sometime." Using someone's name during the exchange should provide ample opportunity to connect something to that person you can recall at a later date.

- **Extend your hand**- If you cannot recall someone's name promptly extend your hand and say your name. This will generally prompt the person to reply and say his or her name.

- **Make a movie** - Try to associate someone with either a character or movie star. You can also think of a visual image which helps recall pictures in the mind's eye. I have a friend with the last name Gray. I can easily associate his last name with the color gray or the television show, *Grey's Anatomy.*

- **Spell the name**- If you are having a difficult time catching an unfamiliar name, ask your new friend to spell it. Foreign names can be especially difficult to pick up, and people will appreciate you taking the time to spell and say their name correctly.

- **Business card**- When someone offers you their business card, take a moment to really look at the card and study the name saying it silently to yourself. If you can read their name tag, focus back and forth a few times on their name and then face. When you return to your office, be sure to make notes that will help you remember this person on future occasions. Today's database systems make it easy to record notes to help remember special traits about a new contact.

Finally, if all the above techniques have failed, and you simply can't recall a name,

• **Fess up** – If you see someone and cannot remember their name after a little while simply say, "I know that we have met, please remind me of your name." or "It is so great to see you. I recognize your face but your name escapes me." This way you are acknowledging that you do recognize them; you just need some help connecting the dots.

Physical Appearance

In today's global economy, business competition is tough. We are competing for jobs every day, both at home and abroad. How often do you call a company for technical support and find yourself speaking with someone in another country? With so many jobs outsourced overseas, it is more important than ever to project a professional image to get the job you want—including how you dress.

Does your appearance indicate you're a professional, or do you need to make some adjustments to truly reflect the perception you want others to have of you? Today's co-worker or client could be tomorrow's boss. Part of a first impression is your overall packaging. Is your package in a plain brown wrapper, or is it gift-wrapped? What does your appearance say about you?

The $60,000 Clothing Choice

A colleague told me a personal story about the impact of clothing choices. After much preparation, she entered the boardroom of a potential client who worked in the financial sector, known for abiding by the strictest guidelines for professional attire. She quickly realized that although she was professionally dressed, she was not wearing a traditional navy, black or gray suit to reflect this conservative culture. She immediately felt a sense of disconnection, and she knew right away the $60,000 account would not be hers. The prospects didn't really care if she was the best qualified. She had neglected to consider their corporate culture thus she didn't *feel* like the best fit.

Give your wardrobe a reality check. Ask yourself, are my clothes appropriate for:

- My job or the job that I want?
- The type of company that I work for?
- My company's dress-code policy?
- The event or activity?
- This region of the country or the world?

In business, it is best to err on the side of formality and wear conservative attire.

Business Casual

Business casual is an often misunderstood term. Your office manager can explain what is acceptable. If there is no one to consult, consider business casual one step below professional dress. An example for men would be a pair of khaki pants and a collared shirt and for women, a collared shirt with a skirt or slacks.

Typically items such as low-cut blouses, halters, Capri-style pants, jeans and open-toed shoes do not project a professional image and are still frowned upon in the workplace. Even if your company allows you to wear jeans, is this the professional image you want to project? Be sure to give it some thought.

After college, I was working as an administrative assistant for a new hotel. One day, the Director of Sales from another hotel came for a tour. When she arrived, I remember thinking, *What a sharp lady, I would like to be like her one day.*

About two weeks later, she called and asked if I knew anyone who would be interested in filling a sales position in her department. I replied, "I might be interested."

I later found out she had called with the intent to hire me. Ironically, a few years later, when life gave us different roles, she worked for me, and we are still great friends today. The point to this story:

be sure to dress in a manner that reflects the job you want. You never know who might be your future boss.

Accessories

Are your accessories too big, too bold or too bright? Accessories should be quality items that enhance your outfit, not overpower it. Over-accessorizing is a distraction and may lead people to focus more on the jewelry than you. This means no long nails with designs on them, chunky jewelry or scarves that overwhelm the outfit.

Bottom line: if you are not sure if you are in compliance with your company's dress code, just ask. It is better to ask than to have it brought your attention. You want the right attention. Ignorance is not bliss.

SUMMARY

- It takes three to five seconds to make a first impression.
- Handshake: two to three firm, smooth pumps.
- Eye contact: 40 to 60 percent during a conversation helps you connect effectively.
- When initiating small talk, begin in a relaxed way.
- Dress for the job you want and always wear a smile.

Chapter 3

Job Search

Out savvy the competition by following the three Cs: Confidence, Courtesy and Common Sense.

— Dallas Teague-Snider, CMP
Founder & President of Make Your Best Impression

You might wonder why calls are not pouring forth in response to your impressive resume. The truth is, with the fluctuating economy and recent job layoffs, there is a surplus of qualified job applicants in today's market. In addition to placement agencies and industry-focused job boards, technology has made the job search easier with websites like *Monster.com* and *CareerBuilder.com* to help broaden your search.

Networking

A woman I know was interested in finding a position at one of the largest employers in the state. By chance, she was introduced to someone at a neighbor's house who worked at that organization.

When he learned of her interest, he offered to provide a contact for her. He gave her his office phone number and told her to call him the next day to get the contact's information. Even though he volunteered to help, she never called him— she said she thought she'd be imposing. She never did get a job there.

—Wendy Gelberg, Gentle Job Search

Networking is a key strategy to help you secure an interview. Online networking can provide access to hidden job markets and help you connect with a lot of people in a relatively short time. Still, the value of making new face-to-face connections cannot be overstated. When you are looking for a job, be sure to get out and about in your community. Attend social and business networking events where you are likely to make valuable connections.

For online opportunities, *LinkedIn* and other professional networking sites allow you to find groups with similar interests. *Facebook*, *Twitter* and other social sites can also help you connect with old friends and make new ones. It has been amazing to connect with people I have not seen for over 20 years. Just keep in mind that everything you post online will reflect on your character and professionalism.

At a lunch meeting, we were discussing social media in marketing, and a colleague told me that he saw a photo of me on *Facebook*—bikini clad on the beach with my girlfriends. While tasteful and fun, the photos were inappropriate for business. I quickly adjusted my settings, so only I could view photos posted by my friends.

You can use these tools to connect with other professionals, develop your networks and create advocates for your job search.

Employers will research candidates, and anything can be used to support or discredit you. Word to the wise, don't lose your head when you blog or post anything to the web. Don't forget to Google yourself. Type your name in parenthesis *(Dallas Teague-Snider)* and see what pops up about you in cyberspace. If there is something unflattering, you can address it before it becomes an issue. Be proactive.

Remember, networking can only benefit you if you follow up. Be sure to contact a new lead promptly or suffer the fate of the woman mentioned earlier who was afraid to "impose" on her new friend. Too bad she didn't realize that by failing to follow up, she robbed the kind fellow of a chance to feel good about helping someone and withheld her talents from a company that may have needed her.

When NOT to Network

It was my first really big hotel sales job, and I was eager to take on the challenge. So eager, I didn't fully appreciate what a true challenge it would be. Being the transient sales manager for a convention hotel that was under major renovations was not an easy undertaking. My job was to go out and make 30 outside sales calls per week to convince the local businesses that we were the hotel of choice for their out-of-town travelers. Never mind the noisy jack hammers destroying the lobby or the inconvenience. We were so sure that we were the right hotel we didn't even offer a discount during this period. I dreamed of working my way up to group sales—they really had it made.

One day, my boss asked me to escort our newest colleague (a group sales manager) on a tour of the area hotels. It is always important to know your competition and understand your market.

At our last stop, my colleague excused himself for a moment, and I found myself standing beside two ladies seated at a registration table. I opened a friendly conversation with them and asked about their event. I commented that we were with Hotel (X), and I was showing my new colleague the area hotels. I asked how their event was going and agreed that this was indeed a lovely hotel. Near the end of our exchange, I invited them to come for a tour of our hotel's renovation. I handed them my card, and we left.

Just as I was getting back into the mound of paperwork on my desk, my boss called me into his office. I wasn't exactly sure, but I knew something was wrong.

"Dallas, I just got a call from the (Y) Hotel, and you are banned from now on. It seems that the ladies you were speaking to told the Director of Sales that you were there soliciting business."

I was not trying to solicit business. I was just trying to be nice.

The take away is this—when at a competitor's location, do not hand out your business card to one of their clients.

I will share more about networking protocols in Chapter 14.

Resumes

What is on your resume? You can no longer use a "one resume fits all" strategy. Be sure your resume includes the key words that are listed in the specific job posting. If a company says their ideal candidate is someone with technology sales experience, be sure to adjust your resume to contain those key words. This, of course, only applies to the skills that you already have, not skills you hope acquire by the time you secure an interview.

Most companies request resumes be emailed or faxed. Your "electronic resume" will be scanned or go directly into a database searched by HR professionals. Just like when you search the Internet, HR managers search the resume database for keywords that are reflected in the job description to fill a vacancy.

To prepare an outstanding, dynamic resume, hire a professional resume writer. It's well worth the investment.

Electronic scan systems and database search systems vary, so always use the company's preferred application format. It may take longer than the copy/paste route, but if their system is attuned to a format, it is wise to use it. Don't let technology eliminate you from the process. It is important that you demonstrate the attention to detail they expect from the right candidate. As you can imagine, they will find loads of other resumes along with yours. You want to demonstrate your ability to take direction and follow the guidelines as requested, either on-line or via mail.

Whether a resume is electronically submitted or printed, the same standards of truthfulness apply. After signing the application form, you are legally responsible for the accuracy and truthfulness of the information. If it's later discovered you falsified any infor-mation, this may lead to your termination. Always be truthful.

Tips for College Students

Much like a screen actor's reel, your resume is your persuasive piece to open the door to the next step—the interview. Don't wait until your senior year to start your job search. Begin to develop your professional network the day you arrive on campus. If you wait until graduation, you are two steps behind your more savvy classmates. Today's market requires that you build connections today for tomorrow's job needs.

Brainstorm a list of contacts, both personal and professional: friends, co-workers, other students, faculty members and your advisor or school counselor. Doing research demonstrates your genuine interest in the field and identifies questions you may ask a potential employer.

Chapter 4

Interview Etiquette

Once you get an interview, it's up to you to put your social skills to work and let your potential employer see you as an asset to the organization.

Pre-interview activities

While other applicants may be just as qualified, preparation will distinguish the best from the rest. There is no excuse for being unprepared. Do your homework and research the company's history before the interview. Be aware of the corporate vision and philanthropic efforts. Ask current employees, or others who have first-hand knowledge, about the corporate culture to get a sense of the company's DNA or "heart." You may decide in the discovery phase that the company is not the best fit for you.

By interview time, the company should already have a copy of your resume, no longer than two pages, printed on professional resume paper.

Bring at least two extra copies to the interview and refer to it for questions about your work history. If you know your interview will be before a panel, take additional copies, so all the interviewers have one. This will show that you have anticipated a potential need in an organized manner. Your thoughtfulness and attention to detail will be noticed.

Arrive at least 15 minutes prior to your scheduled interview time, dressed professionally appropriate. If you have a business card, offer it to the receptionist and politely announce you are there for an interview. Go the restroom to check your appearance and make any necessary adjustments. Ladies, always wear hosiery and be sure to bring an additional pair in your handbag. A run in your hose will not enhance your professional image. Have clear nail polish on hand for a quick fix to stop a run. It is also wise to have a stain removing pen in your briefcase to address any last minute spills. The prepared are never flustered. They have a solution to the "what if's" of the day.

To convey assertiveness and leadership, greet the interviewer with a firm handshake. Make eye-to-eye contact and offer a friendly, "Hello." Do not use, "Hi," as this greeting is too informal for this situation. You may also say, "Good morning (afternoon or evening). It is a pleasure to meet you."

Listen attentively to the questions posed by the interviewer. Respond with clear, concise, well-organized statements. When the interviewer asks you about yourself, be sure to mention your goals (both set and achieved), hobbies and interests. Avoid mentioning your personal life and never reveal your weaknesses. Avoid interrupting. Keep your personal belongings with you and away from the interviewer's desk. If you are invited to show examples of your work, you may ask permission to place samples on the desk.

Prepare a list of questions for the interview. You want to have an understanding of the company's working hours, dress code, ethics, future growth opportunities, etc. Does this job require travel, and, if so, how much? Hold the questions regarding salary, vacations and other benefits until the interviewer broaches the subject. These are important questions, but asking at the right time is equally significant.

Be prepared to answer some commonly asked questions.

- Why should we hire you?
- How do you like to spend your leisure hours?
- Are you computer savvy?
- Please describe your strengths and weaknesses.

Pause and collect your thoughts before you respond. This is sometimes referred to as a "pregnant pause", but do not fear; it is always best to think before you speak.

When thinking of your weaknesses, try to name something that could be considered a strength. For example, if you know that this company prides itself on innovative solutions you could say, "I am always thinking of how to work more efficiently. I don't do well in ruts."

Close of Interview & Follow-up Activities

Avoid frequent glances at your watch but be aware when the allocated time for your interview is near an end.

Common signals that it is time to leave include: the interviewer summarizes what has been discussed, stands and extends a farewell handshake, and/or says something like, "We will get in touch with you."

Rise from your seat, thank the interviewer for her time, offer a firm handshake and depart in a self-assured manner.

Always accept an invitation for lunch. This is your call-back audition. The interviewer may want to get to know you better and also assess your dining and social skills. Many client relationships are built while entertaining, so your prospective employer will be curious as to how you carry yourself in a social environment. Be sure to order foods that are easy to eat. No ribs please! Eat a little something before your meeting, so you are not overly hungry.

You do not want to appear famished or be unable to focus on the conversation. Don't forget you are the prospective employer's guest. Your table manners and how you treat the servers can impact the hiring decision.

Send a thank you note within 24 hours. Follow up with a thank you note even if you are not offered the job. Although this job may not have been the right fit, the interviewer could be a conduit to a better opportunity down the road. Never burn a bridge. Today's bridge to nowhere can be tomorrow's bridge to success.

SUMMARY

- Getting an appropriate job is based on your social skills, educational credentials and job skills.
- Be prepared for the interview. There is no excuse not to prepare.
- Punctuality is imperative. Arrive 15 minutes early.
- Etiquette, such as a proper handshake, portrays your qualities of leadership and assertiveness.
- Be proactive in searching for a job through networking, online job websites, company websites and social networking sites such as *LinkedIn*, *Twitter* and *Facebook*.

Chapter 5

Job Security

Economic times go up and down. Historically, we have been through recession and scarcity as well as periods of expansion and abundance. During times of heavy layoffs, it is essential that you honestly assess the value you are offering your employer and determine what you can do to be the one they can't live without.

Five Key Steps to Recession-Proof Your Job:

- **Be Essential**- Now is the time to be sure to arrive early (at the very least on time) and stay late if needed. Ask others in your department if you can be of assistance. Finish your projects in a timely and efficient manner. Make sure you are the one person the boss would hate to lose.
- **Be Seen**- This is the time to be visible and demonstrate ambition. Difficult times often dictate that companies pare down and let go of all but their best people. Companies that stay in business will not likely layoff their star employees. If possible, determine a way to stand out from the crowd. If you are in sales, what can you do to get your numbers up?

- **Be Your Best Self**- Are you giving 100% on the job? Do you spend time on personal calls or surfing the Internet? The work day is the company's time, so be fully present. A good question to ask yourself—If you had to decide what is best for the company, would *you* fight to keep you in your job?
- **Be Budget Conscious**- Think of innovative ways to generate revenue or cut costs. You may have an idea that can save both your job and your company.
- **Be Valuable**- Build your skills and stay up-to-date. Companies can spare employees whose skills are obsolete. Take professional development courses. Join professional trade and networking organizations.

It all begins with a realistic assessment of your current effort on the job. Are you giving 100% effort to your job? Are you being the one person the boss would hate to lose? If your boss were told to let go of 10% of the company workforce, would you be a "must have" or collateral damage? There are some problems that we have no control over like an economic recession; however, you can decide to be an essential part of the solution.

Chapter 6

Business Attire

Clothes make the man. Naked people have little or no influence on society.

— Mark Twain,
American humorist, satirist, lecturer and writer

I got up early to go exercise before work. My workout would be short because I was the Executive Director of an Economic Development Corporation, and I had a board meeting that morning.

After about 20 minutes on the weight machines, I took a quick shower and hurriedly changed into a suit I had brought with me.

I remembered that I needed to make extra copies of our agenda for some guests. I rushed up to my office, got the copies made, gathered my monthly report folders and headed down the hall to the board room. As I turned the corner, I noticed some board members had already arrived and were taking their seats.

As I entered the room, my board chairman got this look of concern on his face. He came right at me and embraced me. I was taken aback by his actions because this guy was not one to show emotion openly. He turned me around, away from the early arrivals, and whispered in my ear, "Give me the stuff in your hand. Not only is your fly open but your shirt tail is sticking through it!"

Later we had a good laugh about it, but I know my chairman saved me from embarrassing myself and the Board of Directors. The lesson I learned from this situation: Always take time to check yourself, a few seconds can save you from an embarrassing situation for you and those you represent.

— Todd M.

Attire is important, plain and simple. It represents your individual identity and your professional image. First impressions are influenced by our dress, and attire can be a significant factor in who gets picked for promotion.

Gender is an important consideration when discussing business attire. There are several guidelines that are gender specific.

Gentlemen's Attire

Men's traditional professional suit color choices are navy, black and charcoal, or pinstripes of those colors. In tropical climates, a younger gentleman can get away with seersucker. However, this is not always a safe bet. Seersucker suggests a more social environment, so be sure to know the nature of the business function before choosing the white stripes.

Lighter colors such khaki or off-white also may be considered appropriate in tropical climates. Do not wear brown! One who wears brown is considered dull. Never wear brown in business.

When selecting the style, avoid the double-breasted suit for business, as it is considered too fashion forward. You can confidently wear this suit to a social outing or with a client where there is a long-term relationship. Men's jacket lapels should not be too narrow or too wide. Find a classic width that works. A man's jacket should stay on unless the host removes his jacket signaling others to follow his lead. This is encouraged but not required. If you feel that removing your jacket will embarrass you, then by all means keep the jacket on. It may also be appropriate for a man to remove his jacket during very warm conditions. However, always keep in mind what your shirt will look like if you remove your jacket. Will the image of a wrinkled shirt or sweat stains negatively affect your business image and your ability to build trust with your prospect or client? Cuffed pants present a more professional look, but this is best for taller individuals. Shirt choices in white, light blue or power stripe are appropriate. Ask the advice of a professional shopper to be sure that you get a collar that flatters your face and neckline. The collar frames your face and is what people will see first when they connect with you. A strong look requires a tight collar, while button downs offer a more casual option.

So, where can you show your personality? The tie is the accessory that allows men to express their individual style, but it is important to remain within the bounds of professional taste and quality. Avoid loud and gaudy oranges and reds, paisleys and large polka dots. Power tie colors are rich red, light blue or ice blue. Yellow and pink may also qualify, but ask a professional if these colors flatter your skin tone.

When selecting a shoe, the most classic and professional is a cap toe or a presidential tie style. Black is the best choice. Socks should be thin, black and long enough so your bare legs are not exposed when you sit down. Some men wear different style socks to express their individuality. This should be done with discretion. Know your audience.

Ladies' Attire

Although many women today opt for a pantsuit, in business settings a skirt or dress suit remains the most professional business attire for women. With so many options in department stores, it might seem surprising that ladies' professional attire colors are the same as men's: navy, black, dark gray and pinstripes. Choose other colors at your own risk. There might be occasions where a more colorful suit is appropriate, but never during the first meeting or initial presentation to a client. If you decide to wear a bold color, be sure your years of credibility have earned you the right to break the rules, and wear it with confidence.

Ladies save the brown suit for a more social occasion or for a meeting with a client you know well. Brown is not the new black in the business world. Remember professional dress does not follow seasonal trends. Invest in the classics for a professional wardrobe.

The shirt is the second most important item on the attire checklist. Neutrals are best and should fit well, not too big, form fitting or revealing. Ruffles and lace are not considered appropriate in business. Natural fabrics are best. As with all clothing, choose quality fabrics. Retire all items that look worn.

If you must wear pants, a pantsuit is more appropriate than a separate pant and jacket. A blazer is considered a more casual look. Do not forget to button your jacket, leaving the bottom buttonhole open, like your male counterparts. Understand your body type and which styles work best for you.

Find a tailor who can ensure that your clothes fit well. It doesn't matter how much you paid for an item if it doesn't fit. If you have doubts, hire an image consultant.

Hosiery is a must for appropriate business attire. White is only for nurses and not acceptable in business. Sheer black hose is reserved for evening and formal events; do not wear it for daytime meetings. Opaque hose is the most flattering choice and the best selection in business. In the summer, use neutral or beige hosiery. During the transitional months, you can wear tan shades. Who knew there was such a protocol in hosiery? Now you know, so don't let me catch you donning sheer black hose in daylight.

Your best choice in shoes is the classic black pump. Suede is a notch above leather without much difference in cost. Your shoes should always be darker than your hemline. Sling backs, open toes and stilettos are out of place in the business world.

When it comes to jewelry, less is more. Pearls and gold are considered the most classic choices. If silver is more flattering to your skin tone, by all means wear silver, platinum, or white gold. A savvy jewelry ensemble includes a watch, necklace, earrings and perhaps a bracelet. Although dangling jewelry is great for social dress, it will detract from your professional image. A broach or a scarf can be elegant when worn properly. Carry a small purse that slips easily into your briefcase or one that will fit over your shoulder. If your purse does not fit in your briefcase, you can also place it under the table by your feet. Never hang your purse off the back of your chair, as this is unbecoming to your professional image.

More on Business Casual

What is business casual?—Misunderstood. Often it is easy to misunderstand what is appropriate in the business world. If you are invited to an occasion that indicates that the dress is business casual, be sure to clarify what that means with the host. However, if you are still confused about the appropriate dress, it is always better to go conservative and formal. Whatever a company's culture, you should never show up for an interview wearing business casual.

Business casual attire for men includes a pair of slacks or khakis accompanied by a button down shirt. For women, business casual includes a skirt or slacks teamed with a sweater or blouse. Always go for appropriate shoes and avoid wearing sandals, open toe shoes or sneakers.

Regardless of how formal or informal the dress, always keep in mind that you must have a *Professionally Polished* look and attitude.

SUMMARY

- Understand the rules for business attire.
- Select dark, conservative suit colors. This applies to men and women.
- Business casual means different things to different companies. Don't be afraid to ask—it's your responsibility.
- Choose a quality fabric and appropriate color to fit the occasion.
- Wear black hose only at night.
- Clothing reflects your credibility and power.
- Keep accessories to a minimum. Less is more.

Chapter 7

Greetings and Introductions

Bonjour, Ciao, and *Hola* are just a few ways to greet someone. Frequently, a casual hello or even a nod of the head indicates a greeting. How often do we find ourselves in a group where we are told to greet the person sitting next to us or to walk around the room and shake hands with 50 people in one minute?

Of course, there is no true expectation that we will be able to connect with 50 people per minute; the exercise is designed to get us out of our comfort zone and engage with one another.

The real goal of a greeting is to connect with another and share a meaningful exchange. Think about the last time you had a chance meeting with someone that turned out to be a wonderful relationship. I recall a lady I met in 1994 during a return flight from a sales meeting. After a very simple hello, we began a nice conversation and connected, resulting in a relationship that I still treasure today.

She was known to my friends and family as "The Lady I Met on the Plane" until she attended my wedding 9 years later. If we anticipate making great connections, we will indeed build wonderful relationships throughout our lifetime.

In business, making a new connection can feel somewhat forced; therefore it is natural to be reluctant and a bit nervous. Once you learn the guidelines to a proper business introduction, you will have the confidence to connect with others without hesitation.

To Hug or Not to Hug? That is the Question.

We came to the end of a meeting—someone I had worked with frequently over the years, my client and two other colleagues whom I didn't know well at all. The person I knew the best reached out to give me a hug. Afterward, I looked at my client and gave him a hug. Then I noted the two additional colleagues whom I did not know very well. I was trapped. What should I do? Offer a handshake and make them feel like I don't want to hug them? Or go ahead and extend a hug? In a split second, I decided to go for the hug. It was an awkward moment, and I felt very uncomfortable. I immediately resolved to find a way to handle that situation in the future.

Are you a hugger? Have you given or received a hug that felt awkward? Hugging is a very personal choice, and preferences vary from person to person. Family background, culture and environment play a major role in our attitude towards hugs.

In many cultures, hugging and even kissing are quite appropriate. In Paris, close friends plant kisses on both sides of the cheeks. In the U.S., people in some regions initiate a quick hug that is similar to the Parisian double cheek kiss. This, of course, is reserved for someone you know. One should not hug (or kiss) another upon first meeting.

The proper protocol for greetings in U.S. business is a handshake. Not all people like close physical contact. A handshake provides an appropriate way to reach out and connect without encroaching on another's personal space and making them uncomfortable. A pat on the back may also be considered a little friendlier without breaking the business barrier.

According to the Hugs for Health Foundation, proper hugging consists of the following five tenets:

- Always respect another's space.
- Ask permission before hugging.
- A hug is a compassionate gesture; hug accordingly.
- A hug is a gentle embrace, not the Heimlich maneuver.
- Be "in" the hug; don't simply go through the motions.

If you are in a situation where you feel close to some, but not all, members of a group, begin the hello or goodbye process with those you do not know well first. Extend your hand for a proper handshake to acknowledge their presence and respect their space. You can then turn to your friends and offer a hug. This way, no one feels uncomfortable.

If someone is reaching out to give you a hug, and you do not want one, be proactive and initiate a handshake. Extend your hand towards them and look them in the eye. Make sure your feet are firmly anchored, so they don't shake your hand and pull you in for the hug. Body language is a strong communicator and these actions should help avoid unwanted embraces.

Etiquette is truly about how you make others feel. The goal is to connect with people, build rapport, and provide a sense of ease. Be attuned to your clients and respect personal boundaries when it comes to hugs in the workplace.

Professionally Polished Introductions

Relationships are the cornerstone of any business. In the end, we are all trying to do the same thing—connect with others to lay a foundation for future interaction. A well-executed introduction provides a strong base for building a rewarding long-term relationship.

Social introductions are generally made relative to gender, prominence and age. During social introductions, always introduce women first.

In business, the rule is to say the name of the person with greater authority first. For example, regardless of gender, say the name of the CEO first when introducing the new sales manager. Introduce a man to a woman, a lower-ranking person to a higher-ranking person, and a young person to an older person. Be sure to mention something that the two parties have in common and show enthusiasm. Infuse your body language and tone of voice with energy. You can hear a smile on the phone, so you can certainly see one in person.

When you begin a social introduction, say the name of the highest status person first. Use full names and titles, if applicable, and offer information about each person, so they can carry on the conversation. If you do not know full names and titles, just be sure the introduction is balanced so as not to slight either party. If you only know first names, then by all means use only first names. For example: "Mary, this is John. John, this is Mary. Mary and I went to the same church as children, and John and I volunteered on the same school fundraising project. I am so happy to introduce you to one another. You are both passionate about helping others." After that, your work is done; you can gracefully exit.

> **Savvy Tip:**
>
> When introducing a client to your boss, the client's name is said first. The client is the most important person, because without the client there would be no business.

Business introductions require more thought, preparation and attention to detail. There is a process, form and protocol to the business introduction, and if you execute it properly, you will wow your colleagues. In business introductions, always say the name of the most senior individual first. "Mr./Ms. (senior individual), may I introduce to you..." which is the professional phrasing, or "May I present to you..." which is the more formal phrasing. Be sure to offer something that will encourage a conversation between the two, such as, "I understand you both have children who play soccer," or, "I understand you are both volunteers with Habitat for Humanity." It is always best to bring into play a topic that is not business related, so you may need to do a little research to prepare the perfect introduction.

Use this exchange as an example: "Mr. Jones, may I introduce to you Mr. Chris Williams. Mr. Williams just joined our team. Chris, Mr. Larry Jones is the director of international communications. I understand you both are graduates of the same university."

The more polished you become at this skill, the more you will be seen as an expert carpenter in building relationships.

SUMMARY

- Greetings initiate a relationship.
- Taking the extra steps will make it easy to turn contacts into clients and friends.
- State the most senior or important person's name first.
- Be sure to keep the introduction balanced.
- The client is always the most important person.
- Avoid reversing the order of presence. Don't say "introduce you to." Say, "May I introduce to you…" (Think: *Happy Birthday to You*).
- Point out a shared interest to encourage dialog among the parties.

Chapter 8

Electronic Communications

Be sincere; be brief; be seated.

— Franklin Delano Roosevelt
The 32nd President of the United States

In today's high-tech world, email and text messaging have become primary forms of communication. PDAs, cell phones and electronic mail have joined the telephone as indispensable business tools. Yet we still desire human connection, the one thing that will never become obsolete. How do we embrace technology without losing the human touch?

Telephones

So much business is done by phone, good telephone manners are essential to making a great impression. Whether for making an initial introduction or returning a client call, your telephone communication skills play a vital role in shaping your, and your company's, reputation. With less and less business done face-to-face, often, the telephone is your only connection to a live person.

Recently, I met a colleague in person for the first time after working together remotely for over a year. Our meeting was like a long-awaited reunion with a cherished friend because of the connection we formed by phone.

Whether you are placing a call or answering one, never pick up the phone with the wrong attitude. Prepare yourself.

Before placing an outgoing call, make a list of all essential points that need to be addressed. This way, you won't have to call again 15 minutes later when you remember the final point. Have a pen and pad ready to jot down pertinent information.

When you get an answer on the other line, give your complete name and the name of the organization you represent. Initiate the conversation by using a greeting such as, "Good Morning." If you have misdialed and reached an incorrect number, apologize for the inconvenience and ask to verify the number, so you do not repeat the mistake.

When a call comes in, always ask permission before you place the caller on hold. Wait for a response. It doesn't count if you say, "May I place you on hold?" and hit the hold button before they have a chance to answer. That's just rude.

Listen attentively during your phone conversation. Provide information with discretion, and project courtesy. Regardless of how hectic your work schedule is, in that moment, the caller should feel like the most important person to you.

Speak softly and avoid using slang or affectionate terms. Last but not least, smile. Believe it or not, a caller can hear a smile in your tone of voice.

If you initiated the call, etiquette dictates that you end it—gracefully.

"It was a pleasure talking to you," or "Have a good day," are effective signals to close a call.

When a call you placed is disconnected during a conversation, it is your duty to reconnect with the other party.

Voice Mail

Keep it short and smile when you leave a voice message. Speak slowly and clearly. Say your name, company name, and briefly state the purpose of your call. Leave a contact number. Say it twice. This allows the listener to capture the number without having to replay the message. Even if you know someone has your contact information, offer your number to save time and make it easy for them to return your call.

If you catch yourself leaving a rambling, excessively long, incoherent message, take advantage of message playback option and re-record it—no need to leave a poorly stated or unclear message when most voice mail systems have this feature.

Techno-Etiquette

The Director of Internships at a prominent university shared with me about a time she was explaining to a student which classes he needed to qualify for graduation. As she spoke, he began texting on his cell phone. She paused and said to the young man, "I will wait until you are finished."

"I was just checking a phone number," he replied.

He had no awareness that what he was doing was rude or disrespectful and offered no apology.

Cells phones and PDAs are so essential these days, they are often treated more as an appendage than a tool. In spite of their convenience, inappropriate use of cell phones is irritating and rude. Be considerate. A cell phone should never be used where it erodes another's comfort or encroaches on their space. Turn off your cell phone before entering meetings, concerts, restaurants, places of worship and movies. If you must keep it on, set it to a silent or virbrate mode. Most times, you can wait until there is a break in the meeting to respond. If you use your cell phone in public places, excuse yourself and get out of earshot. Take the call outside or to a more private location. Never use a cell phone while in a public restroom. Not only will someone be able to hear your "business," this is encroaching on the personal space of those around you.

Whatever you do, never compose or send a text-message while someone is speaking to you or making a presentation. If you need to send a text, excuse yourself and do it from a private location.

I once had a young professional ask, "What if you are taking notes on your PDA?" My advice, don't do it. You will be perceived as an inconsiderate person with no regard for the speaker or those around you. It is best to take notes on a pad or the handouts given at the meeting. How would you feel if someone was buried in their Blackberry™ while you presented? It is very distracting.

Savvy Tip:

Sometimes it takes awhile to learn a new piece of technology. When you get a new cell phone or PDA, double-check to make sure that it is on vibrate or silent before entering a meeting. If you are unsure, leave it in the car until you feel confident.

Under no circumstance should you ever place your cell phone or PDA on the table during a meal. Make sure it is set to vibrate if you must be reached for emergencies. If you are expecting a call, tell your companions in advance so no one feels slighted when you graciously excuse yourself.

Electronic Mail

I worked at a famous big-city newspaper back in the mid 1980's when electronic mail was still fairly new. One of the tech guys wrote an email to his girlfriend that said something to the effect of "Darling, I can't wait to be alone with you again, etc, etc."

*Though intended as a private communication, he accidentally selected the **send all** button and blasted the email to the entire newsroom.*

It was sent at around 5 P.M, when all the reporters hurry to submit their stories, and night editors login to their computers.

Word of the illicit email spread quickly, and all at once, everyone rushed to open their mailbox.

Suddenly, the system overloaded and crashed. Computers were shut down for hours, and we had to revert to old, low-tech methods to get the paper done that night.

— Anonymous.

In this digital age, memorandums and letters often are replaced by electronic mail or email. Although one of the most expeditious and effective modes of business communication, excessive use and abuse of email has caused certain organizations to introduce new policies.

Social insensitivity and lack of professionalism may convey negative impressions, tarnish credibility and can even cost a company its reputation and potential customers.

I had a different company a while ago, and a gentleman that worked there was foreign. One day he I.M'd me asking me about paperwork that was to be delivered to our client and had not yet arrived.

I emailed back, jokingly suggesting that perhaps it went to Bumble F—ck, Egypt.

Thinking there really was a Bumble F—ck, Egypt, he copied and pasted my message and sent to the client! Needless to say, we were quite embarrassed and apologized profusely.

— L.C.

Limit work email to work correspondence and always use appropriate language. Be professional, direct and to the point.

Leave off-the-cuff comments and dirty jokes out of work-related email. As in the situation above, the foreign worker did not realize that the slang was, in fact, a joke. Fortunately, in this case, the company did not lose a customer, but it easily could have gone a different direction with a less understanding client.

The general rule is: if you wouldn't want your boss, spouse or mother to read it, leave it out!

Be respectful and well mannered. Below is an example of an uncomfortable situation that arose when the sender used a flippant, unprofessional tone with one of my clients.

I wanted to make you aware of an email that was mistakenly sent to Sandy from Jill. Jill was sending the email to S. W., the director of catering, but accidentally sent it to Sandy. Unfortunately, it is laced with sarcasm and is rather offensive—particularly when it was their idea to specify menus in the contract. I am praying that this lapse of professionalism is no indicator of the behind-the-scenes attitudes that we will face when working with the hotel.

SW,

Does $7 inclusive include two dips of ice cream? Heaven forbid we should sign a contract without clarifying that!! And can kids 3 and under eat free or do they have to go from plate to plate and steal off the other kids' plates?

Thanks,
Jill

— Anonymous

Resize your Marketing Materials

I received some information from a hotel colleague regarding their special event for New Year's Eve. The package looked so appealing I offered to send it out to my network to help promote the event. I opened the original document with ease, so I was confused as to why I couldn't send it out from my computer.

Files of marketing materials made for print, such as brochures, are often too large for email distribution. Often, companies will limit the size of documents that can be received. For example, my system will not let me send anything out over 3MB. Be sure to compress documents before sending your attachments, or use a large file delivery service such as *YouSendIt.com*.

Proper Grammar and Letter Format

Just because it is an email does not mean we forget the basics of writing. Proper punctuation and grammar are just as important in an email as a paper letter. Poor writing through any medium damages the credibility of your business. Be sure never to write in all caps as that is considered yelling. Always include a subject in the subject line. Use a professional greeting and proper salutation with a signature line at the end.

Signature Line

A signature line helps your email recipients identify you for security purposes. Unfortunately, identity theft through the Internet is a growing problem. There are even sophisticated hackers that use attachments to plant viruses and worms that can cripple computer systems or access private information.

Without a signature line, your recipient has no way of knowing if the email is safe, as is illustrated in the following example.

A hospitality sales colleague was sending out a greeting to wish all her clients a Happy New Year. This was the email that was sent to her list of clients.

> *Original Email*
> *Subject: Happy New Year!*
> *Wanted to wish you a Happy New Year! Check out my attachment.*
> *Response Email*
> *Who is this? I am not opening the attachment if I do not recognize the email.*

Today everyone is a writer. Think about it. Where we used to pick up the phone to call clients, friends and family, we are now communicating more frequently via email, texting, and social networking sites. You may use an informal style to communicate with family and friends—more like a casual conversation. Documents and contracts call for a formal email style. Most email will fall somewhere in the middle; however, as a general rule, it is best to err on the side of formal. Remember, you only get one chance to make a first impression, so be sure your email sends the message you intended.

Follow these simple email guidelines to help you:

- **The subject line**— Always use a targeted subject line. Do not ask the reader to decipher what your email is about. Most people are inundated with the hundreds of emails daily, so clarity in the subject line could determine whether your email is read or sent to the trash. A well-defined subject also helps track conversations and offers the recipient a reference, so they can easily respond. "Here it is…" is too vague. "Here is the chart you requested" is a better choice.

- **Make it easy to read**— No more than 25 lines or one computer screen. Use short paragraphs and leave a space between paragraphs for clear separation of ideas. Use bulleted lists when possible, especially if the email is long. Use sub-headings to divide your message into sections.

- **Use bold formatting to highlight the most important points**— such as the first sentence of a paragraph or the first point in your bulleted list, as I have done here.

- **Answer promptly**— The rule is to respond to an email within 24 hours.

- **Use Auto-responders**— Most email systems provide an auto-responder to alert others that you are out of the office and say when they can expect a response. This avoids any misinterpretation when you are unable to answer in a timely fashion.

- **Do not rely on spell check**– Spell check is one of the best and worst conveniences of the electronic age. Spell check will not catch errors like misuse of the words *their* and *there* or *too*, *two* and *to*. Always proofread your work before you hit the send button.
- **Avoid the fluff**– Colored stationary and bouncing smiley faces have no place in a business email. Also avoid using acronyms like BTW (by the way) or TTYL (talk to you later). While these are fine in informal situations, they are not acceptable in business.
- **Refresh the subject with your reply**– In an on-going correspondence, the context of the emails will most likely change. You can either update the subject line or start a new email chain to reflect the new direction.
- **Salutations**– Often people will use "Hi" instead of "Dear" in the salutation. They think "Dear" is too formal. Unfortunately, when using "Hi, Sally" you are directly addressing Sally, so the punctuation rules for direct address apply. From a grammatical standpoint, "Hi, Sally" is the same as "Thank you for the flowers, Sally." When using the greeting "Hi Sally", the proper punctuation is "Hi, Sally". The common usage, "Hi Sally," is not grammatically correct.
- **Signatures and closing phrases**– "Sincerely" or "Respectfully" are good formal closings, but may be too formal for someone you correspond with often. "Best regards" and "Regards" are nice middle-of-the-road closings for business correspondence. "Cheers" and "Later" are too casual for business. Reserve "Namaste", "Love", "Hugs", and "Yours truly" for close friends or family.
- **Include contact information**– Make sure you include your contact information just below your signature line. While your signature line is not intended as a mini-brochure, you can add a one line marketing phrase. For example: *"Helping*

*individuals, companies and organizations make their **first** impression their **best** impression."*

- **Un-send button or recall button–** The odds of retrieving an email you wish you hadn't sent are *not* in your favor —90% of the time this will not work. Do not send an email when you are feeling emotionally charged. It is best to step away and reply when you have calmed down. What we send in an email can last forever, so sit on your hands if you must. Even deleted emails can be retrieved. So use discretion!

- **Reply All–** User beware. This has gotten many professionals in trouble when they think they are replying to one person but instead they reply to all.

- **DON'T SHOUT–** Using all caps is the email-speak for yelling. Keep it down.

Faxing

In most business correspondence email has replaced fax machines, but faxes are not obsolete yet. Electronic signatures provide a more efficient way to do business via email, but a fax is still often used for items requiring a signature. In some cases, the fax machine might be your only option to send a document. Always include a fax cover sheet, so the appropriate person will receive the document.

Faxing faux pas can be a source of irritation. Examples include: sending a huge document or one that is printed on textured paper. The textured paper might not reproduce clearly, and a long document can tie up the recipient's fax machine or use an excessive amount of paper and toner. Consider emailing a PDF (Portable Document Format) file instead.

Teleconferencing

*I interview highly successful people to have them share their success secrets. I had the opportunity to interview a **huge** player in internet marketing and social media who is extremely well known in the on-line business world. She normally commands a nice sum for speaking but was willing to do an hour interview with me at no cost.*

The members of my online community were beyond excited, and it was to be an amazing marketing opportunity for me.

*It was an absolutely **amazing** interview!—One of my best. I couldn't wait to add it to our site.*

Apparently I didn't enter the right code combination to record the call, and it was never recorded. I was absolutely mortified. I sent my guest a message a few days later, but I still have not heard back. The lesson I learned: have a back-up recording device.

— Darcy Volden Hoag,
Founder, Secrets Of Her Success
www.SecretsOfHerSuccess.com

The teleconference is an economical way to connect people in multiple locations; however, with the advantages come some new protocols.

- Turn off all cell phones and PDAs. Disable call waiting and anything else that can disrupt the call.
- Join the conference on time. Ensure you know how to log into the conferencing system beforehand.
- Enter your assigned pass code and be sure to identify yourself when speaking.
- Use the mute button on your phone when you are not speaking. Be sure to un-mute the phone when you want to speak.
- Announce your name, and since there are no visual cues, address others by name when you speak.

If you are leading the teleconference, here are some guidelines to help you run a productive meeting.

- Begin and end at the scheduled times. Respect the time of those who are on the call.
- Determine who is on the call and introduce callers who do not already know one another.
- Begin with enthusiasm and maintain a positive attitude throughout the meeting. Smile while you speak.
- Follow an agenda. The participants should receive this by email prior to the call, so they can follow along.
- Explain the basic guidelines for the call, such as how to respond to questions.
- Make your points clear and concise in an organized fashion. Avoid rambling.
- Be aware of those who are not participating; they may need to be encouraged.
- Pause periodically for feedback.
- Offer Q & A time every 10 minutes, so you can gauge the participants' involvement.
- Before ending, address each person by name and ask them if they have any remaining items to discuss.
- If there is a follow-up meeting, be sure to end the call with this information and send an email with specific instructions for all attendees.

SUMMARY

- Your communication manner can make or break your professional image with business associates and customers.
- Never place someone on hold without asking, and getting, permission.
- Do not place a call on speaker phone without permission.
- When you flub your first attempt at a voicemail, use the re-record option. The gift of delete and re-record offers you the chance to get it right.
- Avoid using cell phones when in meetings, movies, restaurants and places of worship. Please do not wear the ear piece when you are not on the phone. It's just wrong—really.
- Maintain professional formality and decorum in business email communications.

Chapter 9

Written Communications

Communication works for those who work at it.

— John Powell,
English film score composer

In 2001, I launched a public relations agency dedicated to Northwest-area musicians. I worked feverishly for my clients for many months, then, an opportunity presented itself to promote my own business in a local newspaper. It was the first time my business, Brio Public Relations had received media attention.

The weekly paper typically hires recent graduates from journalism schools to cover local beats. While some reporters are notorious for typos and sometimes lack-luster coverage, I'm pretty sure this typo took top honors. I breezed through the article and noticed several people's names were misspelled and one inaccurate detail in the article. My husband came home and read the article, then about an hour later, pointed out the most blatant error of all. The letter "L" was left out of the word "Public" when mentioning Brio Public Relations.

Many people read the article and couldn't stop laughing while, in my opinion, it was nothing less than infuriating and horribly embarrassing. An arts commission had solicited the piece, so I, of course, had a few words with the director of the commission. Her *reply was, "I'm sure the next time she writes an article for me there will be no errors at all."*

Obviously that was not the answer I wanted to hear, so I asked for a correction myself. That only brought more attention and embarrassment to the matter, and several local residents have had their way with the story for several years. More empathetic friends would discuss the situation and usually that would lead to spontaneous word games or meanings which became very funny over the years.

Finally, after I'd gotten over my private hissy fit, I sent the piece to The Tonight Show, *for the Monday segment featuring botched headlines. Going to bed much earlier than 11:30 each night, I've never known whether or not Jay Leno used the piece. But at least the article was released from my files and you can be very sure, I am very careful each and every time I type my own company's name!*

— Janet Hansen, Brio Public Relations.

Professionals agree the art of writing good business letters is fading. Spell-check has made us lazy spellers, and our vocabulary is also at risk. We must make a conscious effort to exercise our brains, so we do not lose the art of language. Improper punctuation and grammar, a poor writing style, or incorrect formatting diminish a professional image. It is extremely difficult to recover from a bad first impression.

As a business expert, I have often been quoted in newspaper articles and industry publications. I have been fortunate. The reporters conveyed my quotes and overall message in a professional and accurate manner. Whether you are writing your own message or someone is quoting you, your business image is at stake with every written communication.

Proper Letter Format

Block style and modified block style are the most common for business letters. Fonts like Arial or Times New Roman are easy to read and good choices for business. Avoid frou-frou fonts. Although creative, they may make the document illegible. For the body copy text, use a 10 to 12 point size. For main headings use a 14 to 20 point size and for sub-headings use a 10 to 12 point size (bold).

On both the left and the right leave a 1 to 1.5 inch margin. Personal business style is usually used for writing employment related messages. Avoid using company letterhead for writing employment inquiries or letters that pertain to personal business.

The essential parts of a solid business letter are: date, address, salutation or greeting, body, appropriate closing, signature, and job title.

Several organizations are opting for email rather than internal memos. Remember, email lasts forever, so don't skip the rules for business correspondence unless you want to stumble up the corporate ladder.

Thank You Notes

A personal hand-written thank you note is the rarest and most appreciated form of communication. You should write a thank you note within 48 hours of your meeting. You may also send an email. However, a hand-written thank you note shows that you have taken the time to do something extra, and little things always count.

The truly savvy professional will keep a supply of note cards and stamps at their desk and in the car and send thank you notes the same day. You can even pre-address the envelope, so once you make a few nice comments, you are ready for a stamp. Now you are off to find the nearest mailbox and outclass your

Savvy Tip:

The savvy professional will adhere to the company's preference. Some view thank you emails as clutter. Attune to your client's or company's style and follow the protocol regarding email.

competition. What kind of impression do you think you make when the postmark is on the same day as your meeting? You will surely stand out from the rest.

Yes, emails can also be sent as a thank you; however, a general rule is that if someone does something for you that took 15 minutes or more, you should send a personal hand-written note. Ultimately, you decide—do you want to be like everyone else, or do you want to be known as a considerate, appreciative and effective ally?

Condolence Letters

Expressing condolences upon the death of a business colleague is a business etiquette essential. You may attend the funeral service, send flowers, or write a sympathy letter. Writing condolence letters is a difficult task, but they are deeply appreciated. The purpose of writing this letter is to express to family members how much you cared for your colleague and their loved one. While writing a condolence letter, you need to mention the good qualities, accomplishments or other essential characteristics of the deceased.

Another nice gesture is to make a donation to a charity in the name of your colleague in lieu of flowers. The gesture makes a greater impact than sending flowers or a plant. Be sure that it is an organization that your colleague supported and would continue to support if he were still with us.

> **Savvy Tip:**
>
> If you see an announcement or photo of friends or colleagues in the local paper, be sure to cut it out and send it along with your letter. Including such a thoughtful addition to your congratulatory note will demonstrate your savvy professional skills.

Letters of Congratulations

Writing congratulatory letters is quite easy. It is fun to be a part of a friend's accomplishments. These letters acknowledge when someone has received an honor or promotion. This gesture is so much appreciated, some individuals save these letters for a lifetime.

Invitations

Corporate invitations should contain the corporate logo or company name at the top, followed by the host's name and invitation details. Mention the purpose and type of event followed by time, date, venue, dress code (if any) and other special instructions. Leave out advertising slogans, and only use corporate letterhead for communication coming directly from the corporation. As a young professional, I sent out a letter for a March of Dimes fundraiser campaign on company letterhead. I was called in to my boss's office for a reprimand, because the format made it seem like the hotel was requesting the donation. Of course, it did not occur to me beforehand that there would be any confusion. I should have verified the protocol before sending out the letter.

Acceptance or Regret Letters

Reply to invitations within one week of receipt. Failure to reply is considered a rude gesture. Once you receive an invitation to join an organization, give a presentation or receive an award, you need to write a letter promptly to either accept the invitation or express your regrets.

Announcements

Announcements are best used to inform others of new contact information, to introduce a new employee, or share about other staff changes such as retirement or death. Keep announcements simple and to the point. It is good to send out an announcement or press release every 60 to 90 days, so your company can maintain top of mind awareness. As Jill Lublin, international best-selling author proclaims, "You want to live in the space of '*I have heard of you somewhere*.'"

Letter of Complaint

Though face-to-face conversation is considered the best venue for resolving conflict, sometimes a complaint letter may be your only recourse. If you want a favorable response, the letter should be grammatically correct and factual, containing all relevant information. You may write letters of complaint if you face problems with vendors, customers or even co-workers. Minor complaints, like problems with new furniture, can be easily handled by a memorandum or email. Severe incidents like loss of a security card should be immediately addressed over the telephone. Always try to resolve the problem in person before resorting to a complaint letter. Be sure to offer a solution if you are complaining about an operational or personal challenge. True professionals offer solutions to problems.

SUMMARY

- Handwritten notes are the sign of a true business leader.
- Be sure to use the best practices when writing any correspondence.
- Congratulatory letters are written to your friends, business associates and prospects.
- Always try to resolve a situation through personal communication when applicable. Don't just complain; offer a solution to the problem.

Chapter 10

Dining

All great change in America begins at the dinner table.

— Ronald Reagan
40th President of the United States

Every time I think of business etiquette faux pas, I remember when our company was restructuring, and moving our department out of state. We had the opportunity to visit our new home state, and we were invited to bring a guest to check it out. The V.P. of Human Resources accompanied us employees, who were brought in from different offices throughout the U.S.

I brought my best friend for emotional support. I had several talks with him beforehand and made it clear that it was a **business** *trip, not a vacation, and that the main purpose was to decide whether I should relocate.*

We were at lunch with the whole group. Everyone ordered iced tea or a soft drink; however, my guest ordered a Corona . . . and he was one of the last ones to order.

Another time, when we were at dinner with the whole group, the V.P. of Human Resources asked everyone after dessert if they would like coffee. My guest ordered his coffee with a shot of Bailey's. I almost died. No one said anything about him or his actions, but I wondered what everyone was thinking.

— Anonymous.

Experts agree, poor table manners can derail even the most promising career. Even those unsavory guest situations can have a negative impact on our career, because it calls into question our decision-making ability. Many employees are forbidden to dine with clients because they lack proper table manners. Executives are presumed to have good table manners. Employees who desire to be promoted to a higher profile or management position should maintain dining etiquette in social settings as well as the work place. Using good table manners will enhance every aspect of life.

In business dining especially, avoid the middle school cafeteria antics of, "Are you going to eat that? Can I have your tater tots?" There will be no sharing food, boys and girls.

Eating styles

In the U.S., proper dining technique is known as the American style. We are the only country on Earth that continues to eat in the style where we hold a knife with the right hand. The fork should be in your left hand with the tines facing downward. After cutting a food piece, place the knife over the upper right side of plate. Take the fork in your right hand and then eat the food with the fork tines facing upward.

If you do business abroad, it is also good to know the Continental dining style, also called the European style. This style allows one to hold the fork in the left hand and the knife in the right hand while resting the wrist on the table. I recommend you practice at home, so when the time comes (and it will) you will be comfortable and confident. This will allow you to focus on the evening and not which fork to use.

Savvy Tip:

The savvy professional will understand and be proficient in both styles of dining so that they can adapt to any situation.

Place settings

Place settings vary depending on the occasion and can give a hint as to the menu that will be served and which dining style is preferred. Regardless of the type of event, remember this rule—work from the outside in. This means that you use the utensils farthest from the plate first for each course served. In American style, the salad fork is placed to the left of the dinner fork, because the salad is served prior to the main course. In Continental style, the salad fork is to the right or inside of the dinner fork because the salad is served after the main course.

American Place Setting

European Place Setting

Seating

When approaching the chair, enter from the right side. Another way to think of this is to be sure your left side is closest to the chair. Why is this important?—To keep guests from bumping into one another during seating. When everyone understands the proper protocol, it provides a sense of order.

Once seated, note that your place setting has a bread plate to the left of the dinner plate, and glasses are to the right side of the plate. Another way to easily remember this is to think (BMW) or Bread, Meal, Water. This will help you avoid those uncomfortable situations when no one knows which bread plate is theirs. You, the savvy professional, will proceed with ease and confidence.

Always remember your host will (or should) lead the way. Once your host has removed his napkin, you too should remove your napkin and place it in your lap with the fold facing toward you. If you need to excuse yourself from the table, be sure to leave the napkin on your seat to indicate to the server that you will be returning. There is no need to elaborate on where you are going—saying "Excuse me" is just fine. If you are in a fine dining restaurant, the server may lay your napkin on the arm of your chair and then assist you in placing it on your lap when you return. If they do this, don't be alarmed. They are not getting fresh. It is part of the fine dining experience.

Passing items

During the meal you may be asked to pass an item. The person closest to the item should first offer it to the person on the left, then help themselves and continue to pass it to the right. If someone requests the salt or pepper, be sure to always send both the salt and pepper together. This protocol reduces the continual back and forth that can disrupt a dining experience.

End of meal etiquette

When finished with a meal, resist the urge to push away your plate or stack your place setting to "help" the server. Simply place your fork, tines up (American style), followed by the knife with the blade facing inward on the plate at a 10 AM and 4 PM diagonal as if the plate were the face of a clock. The "I'm finished" position for Continental style is to place utensils vertically in the 12 and 6 PM position with the fork tines facing downward and the knife blade turned inward.

Once the host signals the meal is over by placing his napkin on the table, this is your cue to place your napkin to the left of the plate. There is no need to refold the napkin. Never lay your napkin in the center of your plate.

Keep in mind that table arrangements are designed for right-handed individuals, so those who are left-handed will have to make some additional adjustments.

Keys to Business Dining Success

Entertaining colleagues and potential clients is an integral part of conducting business—both domestic and international. The place for business dining is generally selected by the host. A host should make suggestions if they want the guest to choose.

For business discussions in restaurants, lunch and breakfast are ideal. Dinners are reserved for special occasions, as they are more intimate and usually designed to build relationships. The roles played by the guests and host are equally important.

- The host should reconfirm the reservation with both the restaurant and the guests before the event.
- The host selects the restaurant.
- The host should always arrive early to be sure the details are set to her specifications.
- The host may pre-order the meal or the guests can be allowed to place individual orders.
- The guests should be punctual.
- The host should make the guests feel comfortable.
- No one should use his or her cellular phone while attending a business meal in a restaurant.
- Always be sure to wear the appropriate attire. Call to confirm the dress code.
- For restaurant entertaining, the host should take the least desirable seat. The guests should sit according to the host's direction.
- Following the host's lead, keep the napkin on your lap after taking your seat. Place it on the chair seat if you leave the table.
- Order the same number of courses as the host. Pace yourself so that everyone finishes at about the same time.

- Ask for a glass for any beverage served in cans or bottles.
- Wait until everyone is served before you begin eating.
- Pass food in a counter-clockwise direction (to the right).
- Only use your fingers to eat foods that *require* the use of your fingers. Follow your host for cues.
- When eating soup, hold the spoon like a pencil between your index and middle fingers with thumb up. Scoop the soup away from you toward the center of the bowl then sip from the side—not the tip.
- Leave a little bit of food on the plate after you have finished eating.
- Maintain good posture at the table and while you are eating.
- Do not order hard liquor along with the meal. If the host offers you a glass of wine or cocktail, proceed with common sense.
- Avoid tasting food from other people's plates. We are not in middle school anymore.
- Avoid ordering foods that are difficult to eat skillfully, such as lobster.
- Avoid eating food in large quantities.
- Stash your purse, cell phone or keys in your pocket, coat or at your feet under the table—never on the table or over the back of your chair.
- Keep communication with the food server concise and related to specific requests.

Although following these guidelines will preclude many problems, there are situations that may require additional skills of diplomacy and tact.

Dining Difficulties

While dining in restaurants you may face problems related to the seating arrangement, the service, the food or any mishap that might occur. With an understanding of proper social skills, you can graciously manage these situations.

- Before the guests arrive, the host should be sure seating is set up properly, so the transition to the dining area goes smoothly.
- If the food that is served is not as ordered, politely ask the server to bring the correct dish.
- If any foreign objects are present in the food, quietly ask the server to bring a replacement.
- To get the server's attention, just put up your hand and make eye contact if possible. Do not call out to the server or make any flamboyant gestures.

Manners for difficult to eat foods

Vegetables, fruits, pasta and shellfish: Eating these kinds of foods requires special skills. Cut fruits and steamed vegetables into small, bite-sized pieces. Use a fork to eat pastas. Unless you can order shellfish with the shell removed, or at least on the half-shell, I recommend you avoid these menu items for business dining.

Cultural variations in dining

If you are dining in a foreign country you first need to consider which insects or animals are taken as pets and which are considered food. Also be aware of cultural variations in eating styles.

Dogs are considered to be a delicious item in Korea and many Asian countries. Cows are sacred in India and therefore not killed for eating. Grasshoppers are rarely on the menu in the U.S., while in China, they are a popular appetizer. In France, Japan and Belgium, horsemeat is a delicacy, but people in the U.S. rarely eat horsemeat.

Cultural variations also exist for table manners. In the United States, Costa Rica and England there is no slight when you leave food on your plate. In many European countries, like Norway,

Denmark, Germany and France, cleaning one's plate is customary. Since dining is considered to be an important element of conducting business, before you travel, learn the table manners and dining customs of the culture you are visiting and create opportunities to practice. Bottom line: Do your research before you travel abroad.

Toasting and Wine Etiquette

Choosing the right wine for the occasion is a challenging job. The sommelier will give suggestions upon request. As wine is chosen after the food, the sommelier should suggest the best selection of wine to complement the meal. You can also ask for the guest's preference. If budget is a concern, the host can speak with the sommelier prior to the meal and explain the price range of wine that can be considered for the evening. With this information, the sommelier can suggest the best wine selections in that price range during the presentation at the table. The host will taste the wine, and with a nod of approval, the guests are then served. Everyone should avoid excessive drinking.

The custom of toasting is a pleasant gesture. A genuine, brief toast is best. The host can began with a welcome toast for his guests.

For those guests who do not drink alcohol, the host should arrange an alternative beverage for them, so they can participate. Although once viewed as bad table manners, more and more Americans are toasting with water.

If there is a toast given to a guest of honor, the guest of honor will respond by offering a toast to the host. The rule to remember is that one never drinks to oneself! It is best not to clang glasses, just raise the glass for the toast. If it is a more casual gathering, by all means go with the flow of the situation.

SUMMARY

- Always approach your chair from the right side to avoid collisions during seating.
- Avoid difficult to eat or messy foods for business dining.
- Learn the dining styles and local tastes of a foreign culture before traveling.
- After receiving a toast, the guest of honor should offer a toast to the host. Never drink to a toast in your honor.

Chapter 11

Entertaining, Parties and Gifts

Private clubs are good venues for business entertaining. Country clubs, golf and tennis clubs are ideal places for corporate officers to generate goodwill with prized customers. Know the club's rules and follow closely.

For sporting events, the host should make arrangements for transportation in advance. The guests should ask about appropriate attire. Guests can also buy snacks and drinks for their hosts during the game.

Another entertainment suggestion: invite a guest who enjoys the dramatic arts to the theater. The host can ask the guest's preference and buy tickets accordingly. The key here is to know your customer and what they would find entertaining. What would they enjoy that will allow you to get to know them better and build a stronger rapport?

Cocktail Parties and Receptions

Many companies prefer receptions and cocktail parties for entertaining clients. Be sure the invitation is specific and includes all pertinent details such as time, location, and proper attire. Guests must be told the level of formality in advance.

The proper etiquette for greetings at cocktail parties is to hold your glass in your left hand while keeping the right hand free to shake hands. You are there to connect with people and you cannot do it if your hand is otherwise occupied. No one likes to shake a cold, wet hand, so do your best to keep your hands dry. The perception camera is always rolling and any misstep can become the main topic at the water cooler the next day, so always behave in a professional manner.

Office Holiday Parties

Do not allow the merriment of the holidays to distract you from the reality that how you behave at a holiday party can either make or break your success. Keep a professional demeanor, and don't do anything you wouldn't want captured on film.

To prepare for the event, first, decide you are going to have a great time. Second, make a plan to connect with people you have not met and expand your network.

When the opportunity presents itself to shake someone's hand, don't let it pass you by. Be sure you have a hand free at all times. Remember it might be another year before you have the chance again, if you ever have the chance again.

Here are some more tips to ensure an enjoyable time with no regrets the morning after.

- **Make sure you attend** – Absences are noticed. If you want to be regarded as a team player, be on time and stay an appropriate amount of time to show respect to the host.
- **Be personable, not personal** – Don't gossip, and don't make personal revelations. Make an effort to converse with people you normally would not get to meet at work—perhaps they

work in another division or department. This is a social event, so be social.

- **Dress appropriately** – Although this is a holiday gathering, it is still business. Be sure to dress in a professional manner, so nothing too low, too short or too extreme. Don't put on the Santa suit unless the boss asked you to wear it.

- **Prepare your spouse or significant other** – Advise your spouse or guest on the appropriate dress and topics of conversation. Their behavior is a reflection on you. Make a point to introduce them to co-workers and management. Since this is a business event, follow the proper introduction guidelines for business.

- **Don't drink too much** – Stay sober. Holiday parties seem to be an irresistible temptation for some to lose control. Eat a little before you go and limit your alcohol intake to one or two drinks. This is a great time to network with clients, higher ups and co-workers. Don't blow it by getting sloppy.

- **Send a "Thank You" note** to the party's organizer. A hand-written note is the sign of a savvy professional; however, an email thank you can be acceptable in some circumstances.

Gift Giving

The art of gift giving has been around since the beginning of time. The types of gifts vary based on the culture and the economy of that period in history. Today, we give gifts throughout the year for various special occasions such as birthdays, weddings, baby showers, graduations, etc. December is a month where gift giving is at its highest—a time when we want to show love and appreciation for co-workers, clients, friends and family.

The holidays are a great time to say "thank you" and offer best wishes for the New Year. Although it is the thought that counts, there are things to consider before making a holiday purchase.

- **Customer culture** – When giving a gift to a client or prospect, be sure you understand the organization's culture, their values and customs. What are the legal and ethical guidelines of the organization? Are there any restrictions on receiving gifts? Some companies do not allow employees to receive any gift valued over $25. Others do not allow any gifts to avoid the impression of improper influence or favoritism.

- **Surprise and delight** – What is new and different? How can you offer something personal yet practical? Consider what is popular, like Made in the USA or eco-friendly items. Avoid giving items that carry your company logo. If you give your client a unique and personal gift, she will not only use it, but she will tell everyone who gave it to her. Isn't that a better promotion for your business than a company t-shirt or paperweight?

- **Gift wrapping** – Take the time to "dress it up" with decorations and festive packaging. Be sure to consider special needs for any items that will be shipped. Take special precautions, so the presentation is as nice as you intended. Even if offering a gift card or certificate, do not neglect the packaging. It makes all the difference in the gift experience for the recipient.

What about the office?

Offices vary in size and each has its own personality. You know your office best. If you are new to the job, consider the following strategies until you know better how to navigate the waters.

A great way to give a gift to your co-workers is to do something for the entire group as a whole. You could bring a tasty treat for all to share in the break room. It's a low-budget solution that allows you to acknowledge everyone. If you do have a special gift for a particular co-worker, give it to him away from the office, so no one feels left out.

Giving the boss a personal gift might create the impression that you are trying to earn brownie points. You know your relationship and can judge accordingly. Consider asking your co-workers if they would like to participate in giving the boss a gift from everyone. This way, there will be no feelings of competitiveness or resentment to undermine the spirit of the gift.

Here are some basic etiquette dos and don'ts for giving and receiving gifts.

- **Do stay within your means.** Make a list of the people you want to give a gift and determine how much you can spend. This will help you avoid the post-holiday money melt down.
- **Don't say "I will have something for you tomorrow"** if someone gives you an unexpected gift. Just be gracious and thankful. They wanted to give you a gift. Don't make it so awkward they wish they hadn't.
- **Do include a gift receipt when available.** This shows you are aware there may be a need to exchange the gift, and you are thoughtful enough to make it easy. Truly a gift with no strings.
- **Do give gifts to others who do not celebrate the same holidays.** It is always nice to feel important. Just be sure to stress the gift is in appreciation and not because of a religious holiday.
- **Do give a gift to a special colleague away from the office.** You do not want to make others feel left out.
- **Do participate with a group gift to the boss** if that option is available and your budget allows.
- **Do consider a gift card as a nice option.** You can purchase gifts cards in varying amounts based on your budget, and the recipient will appreciate the flexibility.
- **Don't give items that could raise moral questions** or appear to have a romantic motive. At the office, this is professional suicide.
- **Don't re-gift.** It is dishonest, and you will get caught. It is best just to not give a gift than to re-gift.
- **Do remember the reason for the season** and focus on what is most important: friends, family and relationships.

Home Entertaining

During my tenure at the Greater Birmingham Convention and Visitors' Bureau, my boss would occasionally host a business dinner in her home catered by a local company. This provided a wonderful atmosphere and created an evening that was much more memorable than if we had hosted at a local restaurant.

Entertaining customers at home makes them feel special. Home entertaining is a personal affair, so consider your guest list carefully. Visiting your home allows others to know you on a deeper level.

I would not recommend hosting a business meal in your home if you have to be the cook as well as the host—a person cannot be two places at one time. A home environment promotes a more personal encounter, so don't counteract your effort by spending the evening in the kitchen. This would be futile. Hosting a client in your home with catering assistance can be a powerful way to connect on a deeper level and build goodwill.

Entertaining International Visitors

For successful competition in global market, entertaining international visitors is very important. Building these personal relationships can boost your business. A personal invitation to visit your home is a warm gesture. When entertaining international clients, you should know their tastes and preferences, both cultural and personal. For example, it would be an error to serve beef to a visitor from India where cows are sacred and not eaten.

There are several ways to conduct research while planning for your guest. Remember, a much greater effort is required to prepare for your international guests, and this should not be taken lightly.

SUMMARY

- Keep your professional decorum at holiday parties. Have fun. Stay sober.
- Giving the boss a gift jointly from all of the staff is easier on the budget and avoids resentment and competition among employees.
- Consider entertaining in your home to build a stronger rapport. Be sure you can dedicate attention to your guests and not be distracted.

Chapter 12

Lagniappe Service

For all my fellow Gulf Coast natives, the word "lagniappe" needs no introduction. For those not familiar with this term, lagniappe means "a little something extra." I challenge you to adopt this concept as a rule-of-thumb in your professional and personal life.

The little things *do* count. Think back to a time when someone spontaneously did a little extra or went out of their way to do something for you without expecting anything in return. I would venture to say this action made you feel important. You can engender this feeling in others by treating them with respect, dignity and honor.

How do you offer Lagniappe-style service? Lagniappe is a mindset and a way of being. Shifting your complete focus to another individual generates feelings of confidence and trust. Once you establish trust, a relationship can begin to grow, either personally or professionally. Your personal "Lagniappe" brand will be a platform that supports you throughout your career.

Attention to Detail

A hotel industry colleague shared with me a mistake that follows him to this day. Often in sales we find ourselves in a pickle even when we have done everything (so we think) in our power to make sure things are done right. One day, this colleague had to send a proposal to an important client. This client happened to work for an overnight delivery service. The hotel professional sent the proposal overnight express, and the proposal was on its way to the client.

The following day, the client called the Director to complain that although he did receive the package, it was delivered by his company's competitor. The hotel professional failed to make sure he took the extra effort to send it via the client's company. This left an unflattering perception. In fact, that client stated that had his boss received it, the hotel would not have won the business.

Be sure to check every aspect of your presentation to be sure your Lagniappe Service is sending the right message. Remember in the corporate jungle, it is not the lions and tigers that will kill you—it's the mosquitoes.

Let's see how we can use the concept of Lagniappe Service in two distinct business situations.

Lagniappe Service When You Receive a Visitor at Your Place of Business

- Prior to the meeting, forward all calls so you will not be disturbed.
- Once your guest enters the room, close the door to avoid distractions.
- Pre-arrange the seating so you can sit corner-to-corner with your guest. Be sure that there are no barriers unless, of course, you are still evaluating the relationship.
- When your guest arrives, offer a beverage such as coffee or tea. This shows hospitality. However, a savvy professional will

graciously decline. An unfortunate spill would not enhance one's professional image.

- Initiate small talk and avoid anything potentially controversial.
- Be aware of body language; use mirroring to connect. Match the pace, word use, tone and inflection of the guest.
- Ask open-ended questions that will put your guest at ease and help build a better rapport.
- Maintain level-to-level seating or standing positions.
- Do not check email, sign documents or do any other office task. Your guest should have your undivided attention during the meeting.

Lagniappe Service When You Are Making a Sales Call

- Before the meeting, go to the restroom to check attire and grooming, etc. Remember you have three to five seconds to make a first impression.
- Greet the receptionist in a friendly manner and present your business card.
- While waiting in the reception area, be sure to move your briefcase or portfolio to your left side, so you will be ready to shake hands.
- Graciously follow your host to the meeting room.
- Only bring in items that pertain to this particular meeting. Leave other materials in your car.
- Wait until your host is seated first.
- You can choose to sit either across from the host or at an angular position. The angular position is more open and will foster growth in the relationship.
- Business cards are generally exchanged before the meeting. Have them out to reference during the meeting. This is helpful when there are multiple participants.

- Use professional words that project confidence such as, "Hello" rather than, "Hi," or, "I look forward to hearing from you." rather than, "I hope to hear from you."
- Be sure to offer a handshake upon the initial introduction and also at the close of the meeting.

By practicing these guidelines you are well on your way to Lagniappe Service—*a little something extra.*

Chapter 13

Meetings

*"Effective meetings don't happen by accident,
they happen by design"*

— Richard Bach, Writer

Meeting Preparation and Planning

*I was the CEO of a fast growing marketing agency in the New
York area. We managed to get the chance to pitch for some business at Pepsi®. The big day came and my partner and I went to
the Pepsi® Headquarters, quite intimidating. We were shown
to a conference room, and the client prospect asked me what I
would like to drink. I asked for a Diet Coke®. We did not get the
business!!!!*

— Jack Sims

When requesting or confirming a meeting, the first step is to
determine the purpose. Careful thought must be given to the
length of time, preferences and commitments of the attendees.
Time is something we cannot get back so we must always be respectful of this scarce commodity.

There are various types of meetings, next I will highlight some of
the significant meetings that can make or break your career goals.

Business Meal Meetings

Meeting out of the office in a neutral environment levels the playing field and provides an opportunity to create a deeper connection. Dining etiquette is especially important for those in a professional position where entertaining clients is part of the job.

Breakfast and brunch meetings are becoming increasingly popular as they are easier on the budget. The person issuing the invitation should always pay the bill including the tip. If you elect to invite a client to dinner, expect this to be more formal in nature. Do not plan a dinner meeting if you are rushed for time. Your client will feel the tension and this will lead to a bad experience. Be sure to always send a thank you note within 48 hours. Refer back to Chapters 10 and 11 for more details and tips.

Conventions

How do you fireproof your career? Or perhaps the question should be: how do you fire up your career? Conventions are an effective way to connect with other professionals with similar interests. Even with the advent of social networking sites and on-line connections, there is still nothing more fulfilling than the personal connections you can build at face-to-face events.

As someone who has been in the meeting and event industry for the last 20 years, I can attest that there is a professional or social organization for every profession, interest or hobby. Every contact you make is worth 10,000 contacts. Someone you meet today may be the link to your future success.

Conventions provide a wonderful resource for continuing education. Whatever you do, never stop learning. A great way to get involved and meet people is to volunteer for a board or committee position. This is a wonderful way for other professionals to get to know you. Working with teams on projects, fundraisers and other committees will allow others to see your true character. Again, this goes back to Lagniappe Service.

Conventions are often planned in advance and last, on average, three to four days including travel time. Keep in mind that while merriment is often a convention theme, your conduct is a reflection of you and your organization. Therefore, you must maintain a professional demeanor. Party and drink in moderation. You are a walking billboard. What does your message say?

Virtual Meetings

Virtual meetings are a cost-effective means to connect in this global, digital marketplace. Meeting via computer, telephone or satellite, virtual meetings reduce travel costs associated with traditional meetings.

Some employees feel more comfortable and free in expressing their feelings and views, which can be a plus or a drawback. Without the nonverbal communication available in face-to-face meetings, some statements can be misconstrued and motives misinterpreted. Descisions are often made at a slower rate, and virtual meetings can often impede developing a team spirit.

Before any vitual meeting, it is imperative to send out guidelines in advance.

Virtual meeting guidelines:

- Respond promptly to questions.
- Listen to the guidelines.
- Avoid excessive criticism or a pessimistic attitude.
- Be sure to use simple and concise language.
- Be prepared.
- Keep things on track.
- Eliminate any potential distractions like call waiting, cell phones, etc.

Multi-Cultural Meetings

Anti-Americanism has been a growing trend, and left unchecked can have long-term negative effects on U.S. businesses in the global economy, according to Business for Diplomatic Action, a non-profit organization which leads private sector efforts to provide business solutions for governmental diplomacy programs and initiatives.

Research from 130 countries confirms that other nations broadly perceive Americans as arrogant, ignorant, lacking in humility, loud and unwilling to listen. It is important that we become praiseworthy ambassadors when engaging other cultures. We must take the time to research other country's cultures and take care not to *offend*, but rather *extend* our courtesy in the international marketplace.

For example, in the United States, we often immediately get down to business. In other global markets such as Central and Eastern Europe and Asia, it is considered rude to discuss business before engaging in some pleasant small talk.

Each country has its own essential rules about timing, proper attire and behavior. Do your research in advance so you do not unintentionally offend someone and impede the relationship. Learn about the language, cultural variations and relevant nonverbal communication cues. Offering a simple greeting in another's language can make great strides to build the relationship. Visit *www.culturegrams.com* to help with your research.

Why Manners in the Office?

"I come in on time, and do my job so what does it matter?" It's a common business fact that it is easier to teach someone technical skills, than it is to manage a poor attitude. How you approach challenges, work with others and respect company policies will have a tremendous impact on your career success. Have you ever heard someone say that they hired a particular candidate because they had the right attitude? I have.

A poll by *TheLadders.com* revealed that nearly 70 percent of employers surveyed said they would dismiss an employee for bad manners in the office. Nearly 6 percent said they have fired an employee and about 80 percent have issued official warnings for violating workplace protocol. Some offenses cited were use of foul language, drinking on the job and excessive gossip.

Follow these basic guidelines for office manners:

- Be sure to leave a workspace as you found it or better. If you are the last person to use the copier and it is out of paper, take the time to replenish the paper tray before leaving the area.

- When a co-worker lures you into a drawn-out conversation, politely tell them that you have a deadline and will catch up with them later.

- Put all cell phones on vibrate and only take personal calls outside the office.

- Don't gossip. Gossiping will be detrimental to your professional reputation and damage your ability to gain others' trust.

- Return your co-workers' emails or phone calls promptly.

- Serious business matters should be discussed in person, not by email or phone.

- Don't waste people's time. Avoid sending joke emails, chain letters, etc.

- Don't complain too much. No one wants to be around someone who is emotionally draining.

Treat your co-workers with respect. Basic kindness and ethics are truly vital to any lasting success in the business world. A savvy professional will create his or her own higher standard for treating others with honor, dignity and respect. Remember, while others are being selfish and self-centered, your awareness and consideration will render you indispensable to the organization.

SUMMARY

- Meetings help you acquire valuable information, make favorable impressions with clients and develop interpersonal skills.
- The first step in planning a meeting is to determine its purpose.
- Conventions are a great place to expand your network.
- When hosting foreign visitors, do research to ensure that they will feel welcomed.

Chapter 14

Networking:
It's All in Who You Know...

Making a splash with my internet business, Web Business Ownership, LLC, I quickly became inundated with offers to speak at different events. As a newcomer to public speaking, I was thrilled to be booked for a small audience who was as excited as I was about my topic of the day. I was so excited and nervous that I didn't realize I had forgotten my business cards and marketing materials. After my hour of power, I was rushed by the attendees who wanted more information about me and my company. I improvised, but the lesson was learned in an instant.

— Chris Curtis

Are you heading off to another business event and dreading the schmoozing scene? Do you equate going to cocktail parties or Chamber of Commerce events to the sound of fingernails being scraped down a chalkboard? Perhaps you would elect to stay home and let your career pass you by because you just didn't feel like going. The truth is that your success over time is based on your ability to network and build relationships. What you know is important, but whom you know, or better yet, who knows you, is most important of all.

Many jobs in today's market, particularly high-level and executive positions, fill through word-of-mouth referrals, rather than traditional channels. Keep yourself in the loop and move past the urge to skip networking opportunities. If you are friendly and good at making small talk in social as well as work-related settings, with a solid grasp of networking basics, your personal "Who's Who" list will grow before you know it!

The savvy business professional understands that he must be the steward of his own business success. Check your local paper or business journal for networking opportunities. Most events are listed a week or two in advance, so you have ample time to make room in your schedule. The social networks on the Internet have made it possible to connect with people across the globe.

Day-to-day functions and events at your current job, as well as during your free time, offer many opportunities to meet people. A social invitation to your neighbor's holiday party could be where you meet a CEO or HR manager who is looking for a new employee with your skill set.

Contact or Connection?

If I have a list of 10,000 contacts in my database, does that mean that I have a personal connection with each one of them? A business professional can spend years building their list of contacts; however building connections with people is the difference between a one time transaction (sale) and a life-long relationship (repeat customer).

Contacts are often made by exchanging business cards. What good is a business card if there is no relationship to follow? A *connection* is a carefully cultivated relationship, which takes time and energy. By practicing the Lagniappe philosophy and doing *a little something extra,* you will make a connection for life.

Chapter 15

Presentations

"There are always three speeches for every one you actually gave: the one you practiced, the one you gave and the one you wish you gave."

— Dale Carnegie,
American writer and lecturer

As the scheduled speaker for a monthly meeting of a state industry training organization, I carefully planned the details for my program. My *PowerPoint* presentation was loaded on my computer. I had checked and re-checked everything to ensure that there would be no technical difficulties.

Just before I was to begin, the program manager suggested we download my presentation onto her flash drive to save time. In a split-second decision, I agreed. It seemed to be the most efficient way to transition from announcements to the program. About five minutes into my presentation, I got to the first slide that featured a video. The video did not work. The movie and sound files did not survive the transfer. I later found out there is an additional step to move those elements. The show went on, although not as smoothly as I envisioned. I learned from this situation to always have my own flash drive backup.

What makes an effective presentation? It is a lot more than the content of what the speaker is saying. The audience's attitude towards your presentation is shaped by eye contact, gestures, posture, attire, vocal characteristics, body language, use of visual aids, length of presentation, polish, and both organizational and personal credibility. Furthermore, the etiquette and behavior of the speaker significantly influence how the audience responds.

Eye Contact, Gestures and Posture

Maintain eye contact with the audience to appear more accessible and confident. Focusing eye contact every three seconds on a different individual or section of the room makes each participant feel important. In essence, you are having mini one-on-one conversations with each person. A smile will also communicate confidence and let them know you are delighted to be there.

Gestures can be used deliberately to add intensity and help illustrate a point. Natural and relaxed movements convey self-confidence. However, nervous gestures such as fidgeting, shifting weight from side to side, or clutching the sides of the podium are distracting and should be avoided. Leaning on the podium suggests that the speaker is informal, lacks forcefulness, or is extremely nervous. Don't hide behind the podium!

An upright but relaxed posture with hands hanging naturally by your side reflects grace and confidence. If you are very stiff it will indicate that you are uptight. Hanging too loose conveys sloppiness, and slouching suggests low self-esteem.

Presentation Attire

Like all first impressions, your audience members will form their opinion of you quickly—in three to five seconds. Appropriate attire conveys the expertise, dynamism and trustworthiness of you as a speaker. Knowing you are dressed properly for the occasion will elevate your self-confidence.

If your dress is too casual, the audience may perceive that you lack the prestige of a professional speaker. A business suit is a fail-safe choice. Men should wear dark suits. Women should avoid bright colors. The term "attire" also includes hairstyle, accessories and grooming. Wear proper shoes and conservative jewelry. The speaker's dress should not distract the audience.

Vocal Characteristics

Varying pitch, volume, and rate enhance the speaker's image and help maintain the audience's interest. Speakers with clear and smooth vocal projections are considered trustworthy and dynamic.

A monotone voice, unchanging volume and emotionless delivery will likely put your audience to sleep, while strategically placed pauses can help emphasize a point.

Speaking too slowly, using improper grammar, regional dialect and verbal "ticks" such as "Umm", "like", and "you know" can be distracting and ruin credibility. Using repetitive phrasing can also be a distraction. For example: "At this point in time" or "does that make sense?" I am not saying do not use these phrases, just be conscious that they are not overused.

Speak clearly so others can understand you. Drink water (kept at room temperature) with lemon to overcome nervousness and to clear your throat.

Before a presentation, avoid ice cream, milk or yogurt because these foods increase phlegm. Avoid tea, coffee and soda. Caffeine makes your throat dry. Carbonated soda can cause you to burp. Another thing to avoid is alcohol because its use can yield unpredictable results.

A voice with a glaring nasal tone can be an annoying distraction. A heavy regional accent can damage your professional image. Be sure not to mumble. Seek a speech professional with specialized training to rectify these issues. Toastmasters International is also a great resource with chapters all over the world to help people develop their speaking skills.

Presentation Organization

The presentation should include three sections: introduction, body and conclusion. In the introduction, the speaker's goal is to get the audience's attention and establish the relationship. Some speakers choose a humorous approach to get a positive reaction from the audience. A speaker can also grab the attention of the audience starting with some amazing facts, asking a question or offering an appropriate quote. This should be done within the first five minutes.

In the body, the speaker should cover three to five important points presented in a logical order. Offering a teaching point followed by a story is a great way to keep the audience interested and also provide a human element to your presentation. Stories can elicit an emotional response and help the audience connect with the speaker.

The conclusion is just as important as the introduction. A good conclusion will sum up the main points, make recommendations moving forward, and leave the audience feeling motivated and upbeat.

Humor

Audiences enjoy a good laugh. In the U.S., humor is a popular way to connect with the audience. Tell a funny story about yourself. When the audience can see that you are human and fallible, defenses are lowered and they become more open to your message. The audience will listen more closely to a speaker they like.

Use some caution. Inappropriate humor can alienate, so follow these simple guidelines:

- Keep humor related to the topic.
- Be sure it is easily understood by your audience.
- Avoid sarcasm.
- Do not embarrass anyone.
- Stay away from jokes related to politics, gender, sex or religion.

Visual Aids

Visual aids help grab the audience's attention and facilitate learning. Most people absorb and retain information they see *and* hear more than what they hear only. Using visual aids enhances credibility. They can also help cue the speaker in lieu of separate notes.

To design effective visual aids follow the tenets "**Keep It Short and Simple**" and "**Keep It Large and Legible**". Use a large font size that is easy to read. If using *PowerPoint*, limit content to no more than six lines per slide and no more than six words per line. Avoid overpowering art which might distract from the written content.

Include video, music and animation to make your presentation interesting and keep your audience engaged. Consider the rule that states, "Every 20 minutes, a presenter should insert something to change the pace." Keep a clear path between the visual aids and your audience; don't block your own screen.

Presenter Etiquette

Audiences concentrate more when the presentation is well-prepared and skillfully executed. Inadequate preparation distracts the audience. An ill-prepared speaker can go over the allotted time and disrupt an entire meeting schedule. Smart speakers begin and end on time.

If you are in a situation where the speaker ahead of you went over her

Savvy Tip:

The savvy professional will purchase a time-pacing device to keep them on track. There are also wireless remote laser pointers with a built-in timer component. Everything you need in one device.

allotted time, you can skip planned topics and shorten your speech to get the event back on schedule. This courtesy will be appreciated by attendees and the following speakers, and perhaps most importantly, meeting planners who will remember your thoughtfulness when they are booking their next event.

Avoid Annoying or Distracting Behaviors

Before you present, identify any behaviors that audiences will find annoying or distracting. Distracting behaviors include wasting time going off topic and using words repeatedly.

Studies have revealed that, on average, an audience can listen to a speaker for 20 minutes, but their concentration can be distracted if:
- The screen is blocked.
- The speaker is using incorrect grammar or mispronouncing words.
- The speaker is acting nervous.
- The presenter is speaking too slowly or softly.
- The presenter uses no gestures.
- The presenter exhibits restless behavior.

Presenter Introductions

When introducing a speaker, keep it simple and short. With a congenial attitude, share relevant information about the speaker that is of interest to the audience. Briefly share the speaker's qualifications specific to the presentation. Examples include the speaker's current position, formal education, recognitions, awards, and publications.

Audience Etiquette

Proper audience behavior helps everyone enjoy the presentation. The audience should behave respectfully to each other, as well as to the speaker. Be punctual, sit quietly in the right posture, ask specific questions and at least appear to be attentive. Avoid carrying cell phones or other unnecessary items into the presentation room. Dress properly for the occasion.

Never openly criticize a speaker. Use your evaluation form to offer your comments. Your event planner and speaker appreciate the feedback.

SUMMARY

- Presentation savvy is not solely based on what the speaker says but also is enhanced by effective nonverbal communication and good manners.
- Effective nonverbal communication includes eye contact, firm gestures, professional attire and a confident, open posture.
- A properly dressed speaker communicates trustworthiness, dynamism and expertise.
- Vocal quality plays a vital role in maintaining audience interest.
- Speakers should make it a point to begin and end on time as tardiness suggests that they are disorganized, inconsiderate and disrespectful.

114 *Professionally Polished*
Dallas Teague Snider

Chapter 16

Travel

"Be civil to all; sociable to many; familiar with few; friend to one; enemy to none."

— Benjamin Franklin,
American founding father and leading author, printer, satirist, political theorist, politician, scientist, inventor, civic activist, statesman and diplomat.

Whether for a holiday or business, traveling can be stressful. Even a normally well-mannered person can transform into a rude ogre from travel stress.

Polite behavior is especially important when traveling abroad. You will be judged by your behavior. People won't consider you may have coped with delays, inconveniences, lack of sleep, and rude ticket agents. Don't let your negative travel experiences impact your behavior. Maintain a demeanor of patience, tolerance, flexibility and adaptability. Regardless of what happens, always be courteous and polite to everyone you meet. On foreign soil, you are not only your own person, but an ambassador for your country as well.

Useful Travel Suggestions

While on a business trip, be sure your credit cards have adequate credit limits to cover your expenses. To have a charge turned down while with business associates or potential customers will damage your credibility. Use a credit card to help organize your expenses and make it easier to get reimbursed by your company. Still, keep all the receipts in a large envelope and maintain your own detailed records, as you will need a second source of documentation.

During business travel, take good care of your health to help offset the stress and physical disruptions of travel. Use the hotel's swimming pool or workout facility, if available, to keep fit while on the road.

Air Travel

Government vigilance against terrorist threats has led to tightened security in airports around the world. Always wear shoes you can take off and put on quickly at security checkpoints. Don't carry any prohibited items on board. Be sure to check the local rules on the Internet when traveling abroad, as they will vary from country to country.

Pack frequently-used articles (laptops, prescriptions, books, and magazines) in your carry-on bag, and leave everything else in your checked luggage. All cosmetics must be carried in a plastic bag with an identification tag attached. You can tie a brightly colored ribbon on your checked luggage to make it easier to find in the baggage claim area.

Inside the plane, quickly place your carry-on in the overhead compartment and clear the aisle for the other passengers. Don't start using your cell phone once you have taken your seat. It might disturb others. Discussing business on board is ill-advised, as competitors might be within earshot.

Refrain from pestering the flight attendants with unreasonable requests, complaining or treating them with disrespect. Should you use the facilities, be sure not to stay in there too long and clean up after yourself before you leave. After the plane has landed, don't unlock your seat belt until the attendants say you may do so. Don't rush to gather your belongings, and always make way for others.

Flight personnel are never tipped, but you should thank them politely while deplaning.

If you are traveling by corporate jet, it is proper to carry your own baggage unless the flight personnel offer to help. Be sure to write a note of appreciation to the person who arranged for the service. If you frequently travel by corporate jet, send season's greetings and gifts in appreciation of this year-round service.

Buses and Trains

Proper etiquette on buses and trains is similar to air travel. Always stand in the queue and await your turn to board. Don't push or cut ahead of others. After you board, choose your seat and confine your belongings to your seat. If you are using your mobile phone, speak in a low voice so others are not disturbed. Before opening a window or lowering a shade, ask your co-passenger's permission. If a passenger sitting next to you is napping, and you know the next stop is his, be courteous and wake him up. If your trip is a long one, you can engage in small talk or read a book. As you most often will carry your own luggage, it is best to travel light.

On chartered bus trips, stay with your group when the bus halts for breaks, or while taking snapshots at tourist attractions. Always be ready to enter or exit any transport in an efficient manner.

Wherever you go, you are representing yourself and your company and should always try to be polite and well-mannered. You could be the only light in a weary traveler's day.

Automobiles

Finally, your client has decided to take you up on your offer and come to visit your corporate office to discuss a possible joint venture. You want make sure you pull out all the stops. You arrange reservations at the best restaurant in town, secure a concierge-level room at the hotel, and verify that his favorite beverage will be waiting in his room upon arrival.

It is time to pick up your client at a private airport located just outside the city. Since this is a new airport, it is not listed in the current directory. You are unfamiliar with the location and must depend on the aid of a map to get you there without any challenges. What should you do?

Call to verify your route, have a map handy, and be sure you understand the directions. On-line map sources can be useful, but be aware they are not 100% reliable. GPS systems and portable navigation devices continue to increase their capabilities even as their prices drop. Make sure you have the correct name, street address and phone number for your destination or the people you are meeting in case you get lost or are otherwise delayed.

Local traffic laws can vary substantially, so learn and obey. Getting a traffic ticket is not on the "Top Ten Ways to Impress Your Client" list. Review maps and talk on your cell phone only after stopping your vehicle in a safe space. If you are in an accident, don't be rude. Just exchange information and, if necessary, inform the local police.

As part of the overall impression, make sure you have the car cleaned and in pristine condition. Just because you may have an older vehicle does not mean that you can't keep your car tidy. Be sure to consider your passengers when choosing music and setting the volume. Ask your guests about their comfort level and adjust the temperature in the vehicle accordingly. If it is a longer journey, be sure to ask if anyone needs to stop, as everyone's timing is different, and they may not want to inconvenience others by asking you to stop.

For rental cars, confirm your reservation. Whether using your car or a rental, fill up your gas tank before you embark on your journey. Be sure you have adequate automobile insurance coverage. Some insurance policies cover rental cars, but some don't. Know your coverage before you arrive so you are adequately protected.

When traveling by automobile with others, the most desirable seat goes to the higher executive or the client. The junior person takes the least desirable seat.

Taxi or Limousine Travel

Taxis are usually available on a first-come, first-served basis at taxi stands, whereas limousines are prescheduled to meet you. Some cab companies may arrange a scheduled pickup. Make sure you have an accurate address or destination name to give the driver.

Limousine drivers offer a higher level of service, and will open the door for you. Do not expect this with taxis. Both taxi and limousine drivers can be tipped if they have given you extra services. Always treat your driver with courtesy and don't ask him to drive recklessly to get you to your destination.

If you are traveling with a senior executive, allow the senior to take the back seat while you take the front seat to give directions to the driver.

Many cities have departments that regulate taxi services. If you have a problem with a taxi, note the driver's name and license number, and send your complaint to the appropriate agency.

Fasten your seatbelt.

Hotel Manners

Hotel accommodations vary from simple to luxurious. Some hotels are famous for their restaurants and well-known chefs while others may feature branded boutiques or performances by famous entertainers. Most American hotels that cater to business travelers will have coffee makers, hair dryers and irons available in the rooms. High-speed Internet connections are either available in the rooms or in a dedicated business center. Verify hotels overseas have these amenities before you travel. If you are not familiar with a hotel, ask previous visitors for their reviews. There are on-line resources that rate hotels as well.

Always book your hotel room in advance. Nothing is worse than showing up at your preferred hotel and finding it completely booked. If you are attending a convention, reserve your room well before the deadline to ensure you have a room at the convention site at the negotiated rate.

If you need to cancel a room reservation, do so in a timely manner to avoid charges. Before you cancel a room for a convention, contact the organization hosting the event first. The group may need the room for late registrants.

Show courtesy to other hotel guests. Keep radio and TV volumes down. Lower your voice while speaking and walk softly. If other guests are disruptively noisy, don't confront them yourself. Ask the front desk to intervene.

You are responsible for your valuable belongings so be sure to lock them in your room safe or the hotel safe.

Hotel bedrooms are not meant for meetings, but if you have a suite with a separate seating area you can arrange for a same-gender meeting or a group meeting.

When you check out, don't forget to leave a tip for the housekeeper. Tip amounts vary according to the status of the hotel.

Planning ahead makes for an enjoyable trip, whether for business or pleasure. Don't miss the opportunity to travel overseas as it will broaden your perspective. The knowledge you will acquire is not found in books. To make your journey a pleasurable one, learn cross-cultural etiquette which will give you confidence and prepare you to handle common challenges with aplomb.

SUMMARY

- Stand patiently in a queue while waiting to board a bus or a train. Avoid pushing or cutting ahead of others.
- While driving in different countries, study the traffic laws, as they may differ from place to place.
- Book your hotel in advance. The most successful trips are well planned.

Chapter 17

Global

"Etiquette and international protocol are not about being stuffy but about erasing the barriers to your success."

— Dallas Teague-Snider,
Founder of Make Your Best Impression

One afternoon in the fall of 1989, my professor announced a program called Education for Democracy which was a cross-cultural exchange between the United States and what was then known as Czechoslovakia. The Velvet Revolution earlier that year had freed the Czechs from 40 years of communist rule. What a pivotal time in history!

Two months later, I was on my way to a country where I didn't speak the language and had no clue about their customs or culture. After two long days of travel, we finally arrived in the southern part of the country, Slovakia, where we were matched with our hosts. They immediately escorted me and my roommate to the car. We had another two hour journey before we would make it to what would be our new home for the next few months. Everything happened so fast, we didn't have a chance to visit the restroom. About 30 minutes into the drive, I really had to go.

"Excuse me; I need to go to the bathroom. Can you stop at the next possible location?" I politely asked our hosts.

Keep in mind, we spoke proper Southern American English, not the proper British English they had been studying. They had heard that we Americans do like to be clean.

Another 30 minutes past. I began to feel a piercing pain in my side. I asked again, "Please, I really have to go to the bathroom. Can we stop for a break?"

They politely looked back and offered to stop for a rest and a Coke®. This was such a nice gesture, but please! In those days a Coke® was extremely expensive and a luxury. They were graciously trying to accommodate their new guests. With my eyes watering and my legs crossed I pleaded, "Can you please ask if I can use their bathroom? I will pay American money."

"You do not want to use their bathroom." Their look of concern indicated that it was not very clean or suitable for their new American friend.

With my legs clenched in pain, I looked at my roommate and sighed, "I don't want to die in a foreign country because I can't find a toilet. This is not how I want to go!"

Finally, the light bulb went off and my hosts replied with glee, "Toilet?"

"Yes, toilet," I confirmed.

With a few chuckles, my hosts promptly took me to the facility. When I returned to the car I learned that for the past hour and a half they had thought I was asking to take a bath. In their country, they refer to the toilet as the WC or water closet. We laughed about this episode throughout our stay!

From this experience I learned, your hosts will do whatever they can to accommodate you. When there is a language barrier, misunderstandings are practically inevitable. In this case, my hosts interpreted the word restroom, used in our culture to indicate toilet, as something totally different. Who knows what would have happened if I had not exhibited the body language and uttered the one word "toilet" that was the key to the mystery.

Misunderstandings of colloquial language can occur even at home. I will never forget when a student looked me straight in the face and asked, "What is a Big A— Man?"

I responded with much surprise, "I have never heard that before!" He showed me. There it was in the American English and Russian Dictionary. I was so embarrassed and thought to myself, *What are they teaching about our country?—How sad that they focus on something as dreadful as this!*

It was years later before I heard that term used in my home state of Alabama!

When you are traveling or working abroad, consider the trip to be a great opportunity to learn something new. The mass media have played an important role in bringing different cultures into our living rooms, but nothing compares to personal experience. In a foreign country, you will experience the nuances of different cultural traditions and values. Be open to learning so you continue to grow.

While traveling abroad for business, keep in mind you are representing yourself, your company and your nation. Be sure to research the business protocol guidelines for your destination. If you are unaware of a country's culture or etiquette rules, this can cause unnecessary hardship that can ruin your plans, or even land you in jail. Making the extra effort will propel your success in the international market.

Dot the I's and Cross the T's: How to Prepare for Travel

The first step is to get all your documents in order. A passport is required for all international travel, and the application process can take weeks. Many countries require visas as well—especially, but not only, if your trip is for business purposes.

A friend of mine planned an elaborate 40th birthday celebration for her husband, treating him with a Brazillian adventure to see the Fortune 500 race. As they excitedly prepared to board their connection from Miami, they were told that they could not proceed to Brazil without a visa. The application process would take 14 days. Even paying an additional fee to expedite it wouldn't allow them to travel that day. They missed their trip.

Apply for a visa through the destination country's consulate or embassy. Look on the Internet to find out which documents you need based on the purpose of your visit and where to send them.

Before you pack, create a checklist. There's no returning home to get a forgotten item when you're cruising over the ocean at 33,000 feet.

Here are some items to consider adding to your travel checklist:

- Driver's license.
- Passport and visa, if needed.
- ATM and credit card(s).
- Traveler's checks and a plan to convert to local currency as needed.
- Health and automobile insurance cards.
- Emergency and on-site contact lists.
- Itinerary with addresses and phone numbers of destinations. Make sure both your family and employer have a copy of your itinerary.
- Electrical adaptor. Settings vary in each country and at different hotels.
- Prescription and over-the-counter drugs. Pain relievers, antacids, allergy and motion-sickness medications, and a mild sleep aid can all alleviate the symptoms associated with world travel. Prescription drugs should be kept in their original containers, and find out ahead of time if any of your prescribed medications are banned in the destination country, lest you get arrested in customs for carrying a controlled substance.

Get a good night's sleep before your flight to help lessen jet lag. Set your watch to local time. If you take medicine, be sure to adjust the timing of the dosages.

In flight, avoid caffeinated beverages, alcohol and heavy foods. Drink plenty of water, so you do not get dehydrated.

Plan all business meetings and functions in advance—avoiding local holidays and festivals. Consult natives or people who have already visited the country for the inside scoop. Also, the U.S. State Department's website at *http://travel.state.gov* has invaluable information and suggestions, including any warnings for Americans traveling abroad. You can also direct overseas business associates who are visiting the United States to visit this on-line resource.

Global Greetings

There are various manners, behaviors and habits that are unique to each country and culture. Do not expect other cultures to adjust to your habits, but rather learn to appreciate and honor their traditions and way of life.

Greetings and introductions are important and vary from hugs and kisses to bowing. If you fail to adapt to the traditional greetings of the native culture, you may be perceived as rude.

Even the common handshake greeting can vary from culture to culture. In the U.S., a firm handshake is preferred, yet in France, England, the Middle East and some Asian countries, a gentle handshake is customary. In China and Japan, one should bow rather than offer a handshake

While making introductions overseas, always use the most formal greeting by saying Mr. or Ms. followed by the last name. Never assume a more causal style by using someone's first name without prior permission. Share some additional information about the newly introduced person to encourage further dialog.

Have ample business cards when traveling abroad, and be sure they are easily accessible. The savvy professional will also have the details printed on the back of the card in the native language.

Men should use a business cardholder and place it in the jacket pocket. Avoid placing cards in the back of one's trousers, as this can be offensive in many cultures. Women should keep business cards in a jacket pocket or in their handbag.

Savvy Tip:
Keep your cards in one jacket pocket and use the other pocket to hold the cards you collect. This will help you be organized and eliminate the possibility that you will inadvertently hand out someone else's card.

In some countries, the act of handing out a business card is a ritual. The Japanese offer the card with two hands accompanied by a bow. In Saudi Arabia, always use the right hand to present a card. The left hand is considered unclean.

You can now see how not knowing these protocols would serve as a roadblock to your success when doing business in other countries.

World Etiquette Tour

Always investigate the particular etiquette and protocol rules of a country before you leave for your destination. This section will get you started on your research.

Asia: If you are planning to visit Korea or China, be ready with your passport six months before the date of journey, so you have plenty of time to get your visas. If you are booking a hotel in an Asian country, don't expect Western-style accommodations, especially when you are staying outside larger cities.

In most Asian countries, formal greetings are preferred. Always greet somebody with the appropriate title and his or her last name. Asians traditionally bow to a guest instead of shaking hands. If this is your first visit to an Asian country, enlist the help of an agent to help you handle local social graces smoothly. Business in Asian countries is first and foremost about building relationships. Gift-giving is an important piece, so careful research into what is appropriate will help nurture your business relationships.

Europe: Visas are necessary, even for short stays. In most of Europe, the proper greeting is a handshake. Europeans are more formal than Americans, so address people by their surnames unless invited to use first names. In France, the person who knows both parties is entrusted with making new introductions.

Europeans regard status as very important, so expect inquries about the prominence of your firm. They prefer appointments and are always on time for meetings. Business gifts are exchanged in Europe only after the negotiations are over and a relationship is established.

Some Europeans are reserved, while others are more demonstrative, using flamboyant hand gestures to express themselves. It's best to be familiar with the specific style of each European country you visit to avoid embarrassment or misunderstanding.

Africa: Visas are essential for travel in all African countries. Many African nations are in the midst of political turmoil and conflict, so it is especially important you understand local customs and have a clear picture of the situation you are entering before you go. Consider hiring a local guide to help you navigate.

Africans believe in strong eye contact when they meet someone. Don't offer a handshake to an African woman unless she initiates it. Only offer hugs and kisses on the cheek if a woman is your close friend. Business cards are important for Africans and using their native language on the back of the card will help the person remember you.

Don't be surprised if you have to wait for your African counterpart in a meeting. Decisions regarding business are made from higher levels, so the negotiation process may take longer. African business people are generally reserved, and they don't expect any personal questions.

Latin America: Visas are required for long stays. Latin Americans may greet you with a handshake, small hug, or kiss on the cheek. Be prepared for hand gestures. Like the Italians, Latin Americans, can be quite expressive this way.

They estimate a person according to their dress, education and upbringing, so wear quality, well-tailored clothing and don't forget to list your degrees on your business cards.

Latin Americans are considerate and will excuse anyone for being late to a meeting. They love gifts of flowers, yet establish relationships only after a negotiation is complete.

SUMMARY

- While traveling to another country, you represent yourself, your company and your nation, so behave courteously and professionally throughout your visit.
- A wise traveler will seek guidance from those who have already visited the country, as their suggestions and information may prove invaluable.
- Research the country prior to your visit, so you can feel at ease and enjoy the culture.
- As an added courtesy, print business card details on the back in the native language. You will be remembered for it.

Conclusion

In this book I have mentioned many of the etiquette challenges you may encounter in today's business environment and offered solutions for each. I hope you will follow these principles so you can achieve success in your business endeavors.

If you are unaware of or ignoring etiquette and protocol guidelines, you are bound to face many obstacles on the path to success. In contrast, if you follow these guiding principles attentively, your path to advancement will be unfettered with unnecessary faux pas.

Good manners pave the way to valuable connections. A person experiencing a rise in her career has mastered the art and science of business etiquette and international protocol. Though at times subtle, efforts of kindness will never go unnoticed and will always serve you well. These behaviors are the little extras that create positive experiences and build relationships.

Always treat people with respect and consideration. When you are serving others, your life is abundant with blessings. With this knowledge, you too can be confident about your future success.

Disclaimer

While some rules may change, others never do. Elements of kindness, courtesy and respect are traits that will take you to great heights. This book is to serve as a general guideline. Be sure to do your own research and have a plan.

For information about personal coaching or to book Dallas to speak at your next event, go to *www.makeyourbestimpresssion.com*.

Be sure to sign up for the FREE monthly tips and take the on-line Etiquette IQ Test.

Wishing you a pleasant journey and great success in your business endeavors!

Test Your Etiquette IQ

1) Your boss, Mr. A., Vice President of Commercial Loans at your bank, enters the room where you are meeting with an important client, Ms. B. You rise and say, "Mr. A, I want to introduce Ms. B., our client from the Wick Corporation." Is your introduction correct?
   a) Yes
   b) No

2) You are a junior executive at a social function and meet the CEO of an important corporation. After a brief chat, you give him your business card. Is this correct?
   a) Yes
   b) No

3) You answer the business phone for a peer and then ask, "Who's calling, please?" Are you correct?
   a) Yes
   b) No

4) You are entering a limousine with an important client. You will position yourself so the client is seated in the back seat, passenger side. Are you correct?
   a) Yes
   b) No

5) You are a guest at a party, and you notice a man who is not mingling. You approach him, introduce yourself and introduce him to others. Are you correct?
   a) Yes
   b) No

6) Your host has just proposed a toast in your honor. You say, "Thank you," and take a sip of wine. Are you correct?
   a) Yes
   b) No

7) You are greeting or saying good-bye to an acquaintance from another company. When is it appropriate to shake her hand?
   a) Only at her office.
   b) Only at your office.
   c) When you stop and chat on the street.
   d) All of the above.

8) You are talking to a group of four persons. Do you make eye contact with:
   a) Just the person to whom you are speaking at the moment.
   b) Each of the four persons, moving your eye contact from one to the other.
   c) No one particular person. Don't look directly into anyone's eyes.

9) You greet a visitor in your office. Do you:
   a) Say nothing and let him sit where he wishes?
   b) Tell him where to sit.
   c) Say, "Just sit any place?"

10) You are invited to a reception honoring a foreign ambassador to the United States.
   When you are introduced, address him as:
   a) Mr. Ambassador
   b) Your Excellency
   c) Sir
   d) a & b

Answers:

1. *b: Clients are considered more important than anyone in your organization, even if your boss is Vice President of Commercial Loans and your client is a junior executive from the Wick Corporation.*

2. *b: Junior executives don't give or request cards from senior executives. Let the senior executive request your card, and only then should you present it.*

3. *b: "Who's calling, please" is too intrusive. One should say, "May I tell him/her who is calling?*

4. *a: The seat of honor in a limousine in the U.S. is the back seat, passenger side which enables the important client to exit curbside.*

5. *a: It's a kind and thoughtful gesture.*

6. *b: One never drinks a toast to oneself. After you have been toasted by the host, it is your duty to respond with a toast to the host, then you may drink.*

7. *d: A handshake is always appropriate, no matter where you are.*

8. *b: This method ensures that no one feels left out of the conversation.*

9. *b: This removes any confusion the visitor may have about where he should sit.*

10. *d: "Mr. Ambassador" to address American Ambassadors (or "Madam Ambassador" for women.) "Your Excellency" for foreign Ambassadors in the United States.*

Acknowledgments

As I reflect upon this journey, I see the path that has led me here and the many people who have helped me along the way. A very wise woman once told me "It doesn't take money to have class."— A statement that has resonated with me throughout my life and one that I hold dear to my heart. This wise woman was my grandmother, the lovely Louise De Angelo Betancourt. For her love and wisdom, I am truly grateful.

An earthly inspiration and the wealthiest woman I ever knew, my grandmother Evie Louise Teague measured her net worth by the quality time spent with family and friends. There are no limits on love and her relentless love will have an everlasting affect on my life and those that I touch. The angel without wings, the late Martha (Mickey) Huff who welcomed me into her home and heart and treated me as one of her own. Her selfless love for others, gave me insight into a world I could not yet understand.

I also offer my gratitude and admiration to my dear friend, the late Rob Stroud, a serial entrepreneur who introduced me to the concept of pure potentiality and told me to never underestimate my true potential. His passion for life and creative freedom showed me another way to think and encouraged me to see beyond what is and focus on what could be.

I want to express my love and appreciation to both my aunts, Joan Betancourt and VeAnn Betancourt Davis for their love and support all these years. As the glue of our family, they are both beautiful, strong women that I can only hope to one day emulate.

To my husband, Tad Snider, thank you for your patience, encouragement and unconditional love. You offer me the creative space and the support to pursue my desire to help others and for this I am eternally grateful. I love you.

Thank you to Margaret Ann Schooley, for believing in me and giving so much of yourself. You will always hold a special place in my heart.

Thanks to Jill Lublin, a great mentor and friend. Thank you for connecting me with Tendril Press and knowing that they would be a good fit for this project. I will be forever grateful.

A world of thanks goes to my editor, Robin Hoffman who saw the potential in me as a writer and pushed me to bring out the funny, vulnerable and personal side of business etiquette in this book. Her guidance and direction made this process a pleasure.

My gratitude goes out to the fine people at Tendril Press, thank you for believing in me as an author and thought leader. I am proud to be among your list of authors.

Thank you to all the generous colleagues who offered their personal stories that added humor and helped this book ring true. Your life lessons offer comic relief and a real world example of what can happen when we do not pay attention to the details.

Finally, I am blessed to have a wonderful network of professional colleagues, college students and friends who understand the importance of etiquette in both the personal and professional arenas. For your support I am truly grateful.